VENETO

JULIA DELLA CROCE

AUTHENTIC RECIPES FROM VENICE AND THE ITALIAN NORTHEAST

PHOTOGRAPHS BY PAOLO DESTEFANIS

CHRONICLE BOOKS
SAN FRANCISCO

For Venezia, which is written in my heart and mind, and for the other dazzling beauty of inviting sweetness, mia cara zia (my dear aunt), Rita Ghisu.

Library of Congress Cataloging-in-Publication Data:

Della Croce, Julia.
    Julia della Croce's Veneto / by Julia della Croce;
        photographs by Paolo Destefanis.
        p. cm.
    Includes index.
    ISBN 0-8118-2350-4 (pbk.)
    1. Cookery, Italian. 2. Cookery—Italy—Umbria. 3. Umbria
        (Italy)—History. I. Title.

    TX723.D3973 2002
    641.5945'65—dc21

Manufactured in Singapore.

Prop and food styling by Ester Chines
Designed by Stuart McKee Design, San Francisco

Distributed in Canada by Raincoast Books
9050 Shaughnessy Street
Vancouver, British Columbia V6P 6E5

10 9 8 7 6 5 4 3 2 1

Chronicle Books LLC
85 Second Street
San Francisco, California 94105
www.chroniclebooks.com

CONTENTS

INTRODUCTION

. . .life did exist beyond Venice, near Venice, even before Venice.

— Sonja Bullaty and Angelo Lomeo, *Venice and the Veneto*

When the wind from the north blows in the lagoon of Venice, you
can see clearly the distant Dolomites rising majestically on the
Veneto's northern border. In ancient times, a ship captain once told
me, sailors could find their way to Venice only when they could
fix their eyes on one of the mountain peaks on the horizon. In this
bit of ship talk is a metaphor about Venice and its origins. There
was once a vast land called Venetia. Nearby, but hidden in the
labyrinth of a lagoon so vast that neither Huns on horseback nor
Roman legions could take it, was an island.

     "Almost in the very middle of this little sea, enclosed between
the water and the sky, lies Venice, a fairy vision, risen as if by
miracle out of the water that surrounds it and that like green shining
ribbons, cuts through its beautiful body," writes Giulio Lorenzetti

View of the town of Vodo di Cadore,
Belluno Province

This is the city that astonishes the
whole world. . . . From that desire to
return to her that all who leave
carry with them she took the name
of 'Venezia,' almost as if she
were saying with inviting sweetness
to the departing guest:
Veni etiam, *return again.*

—UNKNOWN VENETIAN,
  AS QUOTED BY GIULIO LORENZETTI,
  Venice and Its Lagoon

in his famous guidebook, *Venice and Its Lagoon.* Yet there it is,
a fabulous city decorated with gold, arising out of the lagoon, firm
and fixed. We can barely grasp what architects could have imagined
its plan and how, century after century, its stones were put into
place.

   It is believed that the Eneti, a tribe that descended from
the Balkans more than thirty-five hundred years ago, were the first
inhabitants of what is now known as the Veneto. They settled
in the lush hills and fertile flatlands, where they showed a flair
for farming and trading. Greeks, Gauls, Etruscans, Celts, and others
whose precise origins elude historians left their mark on the
land that has more than its fair share of God-given gifts, but the
Eneti impressed upon it both their name and their temperament.
At about the same time, from the south, came the Euganei, who
bequeathed upon Venezia Euganea its second name.

   In the first centuries after Christ, people from the mainland
began to move eastward to the remote lagoon area in the Gulf
of Venice, where more than 100 islands and 150 canals provided
natural protection. The early settlers lived off the land, foraging,
fishing, growing vegetables and fruits, hunting in the marshes,
and farming salt. In the fifth century, when marauding barbarians
began to descend from the north through the plains of the mainland, the settlers took refuge on the lagoon islands. What was once
a small, scattered population began to grow and to build the foun-
dations of the Venice that exists today.

   The first nucleus of the lagoon population was the tiny
island of Torcello, where now only a famous inn, a restaurant, a
church, the ruins of a cathedral, and a small cluster of cottages
remain. In time, commercial and military activity shifted to the
larger island of Venice. Through trade and commerce, the city began
to flourish in a loose confederation until A.D. 697, when a doge
was elected as the titular head of the republic, and the Council of Ten
was established to watch over him. This government called itself

*Only when you have seen the ancient
ruins in Torcello does it dawn that there
is no single city of Venice. Venice is
an archipelago of islands that was saved
from sinking into the sea by a breed
of industrious marsh dwellers who were
at home with their feet in water. When
Cassiodorus, prime minister of the Gothic
king Theodoric, visited in A.D. 537,
he reported that "the boats appear tied
to the houses like domestic animals,
where the unstable terrain is protected
from the assault of the billows by means
of interwove withers. The houses look
like marsh birds' nests and the boats
pulled upon land by means of ropes seem
to be drifting round the meadows."*

—TORCELLO, MARCH 1998

La Serenissima, "the most serene republic." Venice was transformed
from, in the words of Goethe, "a republic of beavers" into a for-
midable power that ruled the entire Adriatic, part of Constantinople
and the Eastern Roman Empire, all the ports of Greece, and vast
territories on the mainland. The colonized submitted to its protection, sometimes willingly. La Serenissima saw more than a thousand
years of remarkable unity, wealth, and glory under 120 doges
in succession until 1797, when Napoleon took Venice and sold it
to Austria.

The fortunes of Venice would have been quite different
had it not been for salt and spices. The early traders took the salt
that formed in the lagoon marshes and sold it inland, fighting
off competitors and establishing a monopoly. In the twelfth century,
Venice controlled the trade of pepper, too, which was brought
in from Egypt and then distributed to Italy and the rest of Europe.
Having been in the lap of Byzantium, the Venetians developed
a taste for spices. After the Roman Empire fell to the barbarians,
elaboration in cooking disappeared in the kitchens of Europe until
the Crusaders carried exotic foodstuffs back from the East. During
the Middle Ages, the Venetians introduced spices that had been
unknown to Rome, including cinnamon, cloves, tarragon, and
saffron, from as far away as the East Indies, India, Ceylon, Turkey,
Egypt, Syria, the Levant, and the Balkans.

The Venetians were, above all, merchants and traders. They
became fabulously rich from the duties and surcharges exacted
from foreign ships that trafficked spices and exotic foods through
their port.

That proverbial wealth, however, did not belong to all
Venetians. It was what Henry James called "the splendid accumula-
tions of the happier few." Likewise, it would be a mistake to think
that rich and poor ate alike. The foods of the *signori*, the wealthy,
were one thing. The dishes of the *popolo*, the people, were another.
Behind the stage set that is Venice, in the back alleys fishwives

quarreled, women in kerchiefs and cheap cotton dresses hauled buckets of water from the public fountains for cooking and bathing, workingmen crowded into bars for cheap drink, and street urchins went shoeless. The foods and spices of the wealthy were luxuries the common people could not afford.

The fantastic cuisine of the *signori* is legendary, but only Venice's poor dishes have lasted. The cooking traditions of the working people arose out of necessity. Their foods were simple and often portable—dishes that could be prepared in advance and eaten on-site at the end of the market day or were ready upon returning home after a long, hard workday.

Mainland Veneto

The Veneto, or Venezia Euganea, to distinguish it from its two sister regions, Friuli Venezia Giulia and Venezia Tridentina, which flank it on either side, has been deeply influenced by its capital city, but it has blessings all its own. Within its borders are rich alluvial deltas, lush flatlands, soft hills and fertile valleys, the largest lake in Italy, one hundred miles of beaches, and one of the most dramatic mountainscapes in the world.

When the barbarian invasions receded, the mainland began to regain its vigor. The Republic of Venice looked toward the territory from which its forebears had fled. It did not want to be dependent on foreign markets for staples it could not grow. In order to remain sovereign, Venice turned to the provinces. Rice was cultivated in the Po River delta, corn and wheat in the plains, and beans and potatoes in the mountains. By the eighteenth century, Venice was harvesting enough rice to sate Venetian appetite for risotto, with plenty more to export. La Serenissima sent governors to the far end of the Veneto to oversee and protect its holdings, which were, in turn, grateful to be part of the glorious republic.

The cosmopolitanism that is the essence of Venice affected every aspect of its life and culture and went far beyond its borders. Through its port came new foods and flavors that influenced and revolutionized eating habits throughout Europe. The Venetians introduced coffee, the table napkin, and the fork. Itinerant travelers by both land and sea, Venetians brought their home with them—its commerce, its knack for business, its exotic flavors— wherever they went.

In Italy, food is considered to be good only in homes where there is an old lady with slippers in the kitchen.

—FRANCESCO ANTONUCCI, PROPRIETOR, REMI (VENETIAN) RESTAURANT, NEW YORK CITY

Garden markets line the Veneto coast and are at the heart of every town and village throughout the region. If Venice has become a museum, the markets of the city—Rialto, the Lido, and all the rest—with their golden pumpkin flowers, their violet-and-green-streaked artichokes, their scarlet lettuces, their coral-shelled crabs, and their other beautiful foods, are its living colors.

The Cooking of Venice

Researchers scouring Venetian libraries have discovered that, since the fifteenth century, some two thousand books have been written about Venetian cooking, table manners, and the art of eating. Venice was connected to Byzantium, which had a highly developed cuisine. Like court cooking in the rest of Italy, the cooking of the Venetian aristocracy was always open to foreign notions—some say, to a fault. Gerolamo Zanetti writes in his *Memorie:* "The French cooks have spoiled Venetian stomachs with so much trash, sauces, broths, and especially stocks in which four pairs of pigeons are so reduced to pure broth that they can barely be found. . . . Now garlic and onion are very fashionable and they go into almost every dish."

Contemporary Venetians show little evidence of the bacchanal eating habits attributed to their ancestors. What is worrisome today, however, is that genuine Venetian cooking, that is, home cooking, has become the gastronomic equivalent of an endangered species. Only 30 percent of the resident population of Venice is Venetian by birth. Much of the cooking done in the city is restaurant cooking, which only infrequently reproduces traditional food. Despite this situation, a number of ancestral dishes have survived. There is a Venice within Venice, away from the main tourist attractions and the commercial thoroughfares, where the local population lives. The cooking in those enclaves is based on rice, polenta, beans, fish, and vegetables.

The city's Rialto market still sells to the locals and to the islands' many restaurateurs. The crops from the lagoon islands—peaches, apricots, green celery, artichokes—are shuttled in along with products from the Rovigo estuary (famous for its "white" celery), which lies to the south, and from the fertile agricultural lands of Verona and Treviso.

The Cooking of the Mainland Provinces

Most introductions to Venetian cookbooks say that the Veneto eats

*In August, James had crossed the Simplon
Pass on foot with "an individual"
to carry his knapsack, then went diligently
"down, down—on, on into Italy—
a rapturous progress thro' a wild luxuriance
of corn and frescoed villages and
clamorous beggars and all the good old
Italianisms of tradition."*

—HUGH HONOUR AND JOHN FLEMING,
Venetian Hours

what Venice eats, and it is true to some extent. But the region's other provinces, Rovigo, Padua, Treviso, Verona, Vicenza, and Belluno, are also greatly influenced by the lay of the land and its natural resources. For one thing, the Veneto mainland was the breadbasket of Venice or, more specifically, the "rice dish" or the "polenta pot." For another, parts of the Veneto were playgrounds for the rich Venetian merchants who left their city in droves in hot weather when the lagoon began to stink. It was natural that a country kitchen would evolve.

The province of Rovigo, also called the Polesine, shares a border with Emilia-Romagna and is close enough to Chioggia to share salt flats. Like Venice, Rovigo is preoccupied with water, but its relative poverty resists further comparison. The Po and Adige Rivers run through Rovigo, as do many smaller rivers, which create canals, lakes, and vast areas of flooded land. This is the Po River delta, prime rice-growing land, and the grain has been one of Rovigo's most important crops for five hundred years.

Since ancient times, the rivers have endowed the province with rich alluvial soil. Corn has been planted here since it was first introduced in 1603, and the province has been polenta country ever since. There is some farming in the lush flatlands, and a cult of barnyard animals, so that the flavor of chickens, pigs, turkeys, geese, and guinea hens raised *ruspanti,* "naturally," makes elaborate cooking unnecessary. The cooking of Rovigo is characterized by humble dishes: gnocchi of potato or bread, bean soups some-times thickened with polenta, all kinds of rice dishes, lots of eggs, and vegetable cookery.

Historically, the other centers on the Veneto plains—Padua, Treviso, Verona, and Vicenza—have been more prosperous than Rovigo due to their greater commerce and industry. This is reflected in their cooking, which displays both agricultural traditions and aristocratic influences.

Padua lies between Venice and Rovigo. The road along the Brenta Canal, lined with splendid patrician villas and excellent fish restaurants, leads to Venice. Padua offers a table distinguished by its superb pork and poultry. Pigs are pampered and fed acorns and chestnuts to prepare them for the renowned Montagnana hams. Padua's proximity to the salt flats of Chioggia and the markets of Venice made the production of this prized prosciutto inevitable.

The Paduans also love chicken. I found this out several years ago when I asked a local agronomist and gourmet I met in Chioggia what the food was like in his home province. "We eat lots of chicken," he answered. When I asked how the Paduans liked to cook the birds, he responded, "in water or in wine." Chicken and barnyard animals are not only braised in wine and boiled, but are also spit-roasted, fried, and cooked in innumerable other ways.

Another distinction of the province is that the white truffle is found there, a good fortune it shares with neighboring Rovigo. Also, it is the only part of the Veneto where bread is traditional. That wheat and ovens were scarce in past times illustrates the relative wealth of the province. The city of Padua, which bears the same name as the province, was an important medieval and Renaissance center second only to Venice in the quantity and quality of artwork it patronized. Its aristocratic past, its vital countryside, and its closeness to Venice and to the border of Emilia-Romagna are reflected in the elegance of many of its dishes.

The Treviso Province is a bastion of good cooking, and of great wine, as demonstrated in the local saying, *A chi che no ghe piase el vin, che Dio ghe toga l'acqua!* (Whomever doesn't like wine, may God take away his water!). In the case of the Veneto, where water is so important, this bit of ancient advice has a double meaning. Outside of the Dolomite centers, all the major cities were established on a waterway of one kind or another. Treviso is on the Sile River. It also shares a border with Venice and has been greatly influenced by it in its cooking and culture.

This is fertile farm country. Without a doubt, the most famous crops are what some locals call "the flowers that you eat," the red radicchio of Treviso and the variegated variety of Castelfranco. Here, the cultivation of radicchio is tantamount to an art, and the number of ways in which Treviso cooks prepare the local treasure is nothing short of astonishing. Its harvest in the early spring inspires particularly exuberant cooking and festivals in the public squares. The province also boasts an old and lively restaurant tradition, so that today plenty of superb restaurants and informal trattorias dot the towns and cities, and many more are scattered throughout the countryside. Treviso is a land of fish, meat and game, and cured meats, and of Prosecco, the delicious sparkling white wine that is brought to the table with every course. It is no wonder that culinary expert Paolo Morganti claims that 50 percent of Treviso's tourism is based on gastronomy.

Like Treviso, Verona is a rich agricultural region around which fine cooking traditions have evolved. Whatever absence of meat there is in Venice is more than compensated for here. Like Emilia-Romagna to the south and Lombardy to the west, Verona loves *bollito misto*, mixed boiled meats, although here they are embellished with particular sauces at the table, including the famous *pearà*, Verona's regal version of bread sauce, and *cren*, based on horseradish. Verona is conscious of its noble roots. The refinement of some of its cooking derives from the Renaissance tables of the noble Scaligeri family, Verona's once powerful lords. The region is most famous outside its borders for *pan d'oro* (golden bread), tall, fluffy, buttery, sweet yeast bread covered with confectioners' sugar. The most evocative Veronese tradition is the Venerdì Gnoccolare, when the entire city celebrates its independence in A.D. 489 by eating gnocchi in the splendid Piazza San Xeno.

Verona has everything that the plains provinces have, and it

FACING PAGE:
A canal in Treviso

Del sen che il lago flessuoso falle:
S'appoggia al piè d'un monte, e la petrosa
Punta aguzza torregiale alle spalle:
Ma le falde beater di vigneti
S'infrondano di fertili olivetti

In the supple arch of the lake
Leaning at the foot of a mountain
Whose stony points shoulder
The slopes blessed with vineyards
And fertile leafy olives.

—Cesare Betteloni
from *Lago di Garda*,
Simone Azzoni

also has soft foothills and the entire long eastern stretch of Lake Garda, the biggest lake in Italy. It shares the lake with Lombardy, except for its northern tip, which only touches Trentino. Driving from Verona into the lake district, it becomes clear that Garda has its own culture. Roadside stands advertise in Italian and German, some even selling *würstel* and beer. The Germans don't have to travel far to reach the Garda area, and they seem to be quite at home here.

Garda could almost be its own province because it is a climate within a climate. The mountains that crown the lake invite a union of winds from north and south within their shelter, creating a balmy microclimate that never reaches freezing temperatures in winter, a condition that permits olive groves to flourish around the limpid shores of the lake. The lake, fed by the deep waters of glacial lakes and rivers that flow from the Alps, is home to thirty-five species of fish. Not surprisingly, there is a cult of freshwater fish here. Based on olive oil, fish, vegetables, and fruits, the Garda diet imitates the Mediterranean diet. On the shores of the lake, among the olive groves, lemon and orange trees, palms, and cypress, there is a town called Limone, where the inhabitants often live to be well over the age of ninety and sometimes even one hundred years old.

Although it lacks a coastline and has no lakes, Vicenza, of all the provinces of the Veneto, is the one most aligned with the cooking of Venice. Bassano del Grappa, one of its most lovely towns, gives its name to the famous asparagus for which the region is well known. Besides that, like Venice, Vicenza is a vegetable kingdom. Also like Venice, it makes risottos with virtually every vegetable: *bruscandoli* (hops), peas, asparagus, fennel, pumpkin, squashes, and wild mushrooms, to name only a few.

If Verona has Garda, Vicenza has Palladio. The most important and beautiful of the sixteenth-century master architect's work was executed in Vicenza proper and in dramatic settings throughout the countryside. To eat *baccalà alla vicentina* in any of the Palladian villas that have been transformed into luxurious restaurants is at least as evocative as a floating feast on the enchanted lagoon under midnight fireworks.

Driving northward from the plains, the gentle landscape gives way to rugged alpine scenery. Before long, the distant peaks seen from the Adriatic at the entrance of the Venetian lagoon dwarf everything within their shadows. The snow-covered glacial rock that juts abruptly into the sky is 230 million years old, a progressive accumulation of coral, sponges, shells, sea organisms, and mineral salts. If anywhere in the Veneto is the antithesis of Venice proper, it is this mountain province, Belluno.

The earliest people to settle in the valleys of the Italian Dolomites were an ancient Indo-European population called Reti or Salvans, who descended from the mountain passes at least three thousand years ago. Mystery surrounds their origins and their lineage, but we know for certain that they were shepherds who were acclimatized to the extreme mountain temperatures. Legend describes them as "a people who offend no one, men who fought only when they were provoked, then their strength was terrible, because they had the power of giants." This would make them resemble the ancient Etruscans, and, in fact, one theory contends that they were fugitive Etruscans who fled the brutal control of Rome. In A.D. 15, the Romans took the Alps, and in time, the Reti and the Romans became a unified people. The Reti left the Ladini (a people, a culture, a distinctive cuisine) and Ladino (a Latin-based language still spoken north of Belluno today).

Belluno's relative isolation makes it a fascinating study. Within the province, the areas of Alpago, Agordino, Cortina, and the Cadore have their own culinary traditions. The Cadore further divides itself into two distinct cultures. One part, the valley of

Comèlico, is influenced by Switzerland, with which it shares a frontier. The other part borders Austria.

Belluno passed into the hands of the Venetians and the Austrians at various points, and it was influenced by both. La Serenissima laid a great protective shroud on its territories. In return, it took the natural resources it needed, primarily lumber for its ships. It left a governor in the city of Pieve di Cadore, who not only met with no resistance, but won the hearts of the people. The locals insist that the Hapsburgs made no change to their way of life except to introduce goulash, but at midday, in the trattorias off the tourist routes, laborers sit over their *würstel* and polenta. Strudel is for dessert, and the use of butter and milk in cooking, and of poppy seeds in baking, all point to Austria's influence.

Until after World War II, most residents ate poorly, and little. The mountain terrain and cooler climate were not hospitable to agriculture, but they supported corn for polenta, potatoes, and beans, all from the New World. It's no wonder that the populace was obsessed with polenta—they ate it three times a day. The wealthy ate it, too, adding various condiments to fortify and flavor it. The potato was introduced in the 1800s. With it, Belluno made gnocchi. Until after World War II, when wheat became common throughout the Veneto, bread was made of rye. Whatever crusts were left were swept off the table and transformed into another type of dumpling, this one flavored with bits of leftover *speck* (smoked ham) or hard cheese. Called *canederli*, they are a counterpart to the Austrian *knödel* and were considered *un pulitore della mensa*, "a cleaner of the table." Meat, milk, cheese, and butter were accessible only to well-off farmers who could afford to keep pigs and cows. The northern part of the province—Cadore, Agordo, Zoldo, and Comèlico—was more prosperous than the southern part, which was largely a population of sharecroppers and laborers.

Considerable space has been given to outlining the culinary

quiddities that distinguish Venice and its six provinces, but it is also true that certain foods, including polenta, *baccalà*, beans, and risotto, are important to all the provinces, and thus serve as great unifiers. The Veneti have strong ties to their traditions. This is only natural where the bastardization of the genuine kitchen by international influences (a hazard of a cuisine that became, largely, restaurant cooking) and the preponderance of foreigners have caused the Venetians to protect their past jealously. How ironic that, with all the fantastic recipes and exotic flavors that the empire once indulged in, only its simple foods have survived. One day, I chatted on this very subject with Giacomo Gregario, a philosopher-cum-restaurateur, as we sat in his splendid restaurant in the Dolomites (the Italians are wont to put their elbow on the philosopher's stone). "Signora," he advised, summing it up, conjuring a distant view of Venice, "an explanation for such an irony can be found in a Latin axiom that applies as much in cooking as it does in politics: *in medio stat virtus*, 'virtue is in the middle.'" Herein lies the theme of the genuine Veneto kitchen: *cucina ricca* combined with *cucina povera* in a blend of rich traditions and humble ingredients.

WINES OF THE VENETO

vini veneti

Making and drinking wine in the Veneto date back to its first inhabitants, the Eneti. When the Romans arrived, they codified methods for viticulture, which were practiced into the Middle Ages. During the Renaissance, great improvements in wine making occurred, as did refinements in enology. In 1583, Cassiodorus, the erudite prime minister of the Goth king Theodoric, wrote an epistle about the wines of Verona. Describing the "purple" reds and the whites "like lilies," he sings, "[they are] of an incredible sweetness and softness . . . an almost meaty liquid . . . a drink that you could almost eat."

The intimate ambrosial wines of Cassiodorus's Veneto are a far cry from the mass-produced bottlings that were exported in the mid-twentieth century. But since the 1970s, the region has made some of Italy's finest wines, a result of a concerted national effort to aim for quality instead of quantity. Laws covering wine making, from vineyard to aging cellar, protect the name and reputation of the region's excellent wines. Each wine type has its own

Vines and cane huts by the Po River delta

Fill the glass that is empty
Empty the glass that is full
Don't ever leave it empty
Don't ever leave it full

—SAYING FOUND ON A DOLCETTI DI
VENEZIA WINE FLASK

Good Champagne is much worse
than bad Prosecco.

—NICOLETTA POLO,
DESCENDANT OF MARCO POLO

FACING PAGE:
A glass of homemade wine at
Le Garzette, Mallamoco, Venice

personality, but each must fit the profile—be identifiable as the particular wine—by taste and not be confused with any other wine. Wine made outside these rules is not permitted to bear a DOC (Denominazione di Origine Controllata) label or the even more coveted DOCG (Denominazione di Origine Controllata Garantita) label, both guarantees of quality.

No wonder that wine has been produced in the Veneto since its very beginnings. Nature has bestowed the Veneto with a lush and fertile landscape that has begged for vines. The celebrated Bardolino, Soave, and Valpolicella vineyards are scattered in the Lake Garda region, producing not only the reds and whites that have become famous outside the borders of Italy, but also lovely local wines that are treasures for travelers to discover, like the perfumed Lugana *spumante,* which is made to drink with fish from the lake. Prosecco, the delightful sparkling white wine whose production is concentrated in the areas of Valdobbiadene and Conegliano in the province of Treviso, is astonishingly good—and available in America.

Lake Garda's hospitable microclimate encourages a lively diversity of grape varieties and inspires creativity in wine making, but the most important wines of the region are Amarone; Valpolicella (*classico* and *ripasso* varieties); Recioto, the roseate Bardolino of the reds; and, among whites, Bianco di Custoza, Soave, and the Soave sweet variety called Recioto di Soave, which has earned the DOCG label. Other wines of distinction are Corvina Veronese, the Merlot and the Cabernet from the Euganean Hills, and labels from the eastern plains that border Friuli.

Wine is in the local blood. Italian wine writer Lucio Bussi goes so far as to speculate that it is part of the genetic heritage of the people of Verona, the most important DOC wine—producing area in the region, a proposal he supports with the old saying, *veronesi tuti mati,* "everyone in Verona is nuts."

THE VENETO PANTRY

Why, indeed, do tourists go in droves to every monument and every gallery and every church, even every glass factory in Murano and every lace shop in Burano, when they descend upon Venice, but remain ignorant about the remarkable cheeses, prosciutti, wines, and so forth that generations of artisans have developed into refined and delicious products?

Here are marvels of the Veneto that can be tasted, no, savored, and some appreciated and remembered even outside its borders. Many of these foods carry the DOC (Denominazione di Origine Controllata) label, a mark of quality indicating they have been produced in a restricted zone. Yet another label, DOP (Denominazione di Origine Protetta), is now seen throughout Italy as well. It is awarded by the European Union and duplicates the DOC designation.

Bruscansi, wild asparagus-like spring shoots, at the Market in Bardolino

Cheeses
Where there are mountains, there is cheese, and the Veneto has its share of both. Two of the region's cheeses, Asiago and *grana padano*, often simply called *grana*, are well known abroad. The others are

strangers to the lips of most outside the area, although there is
no reason why they should be. All of the cheeses mentioned here are
available in America except for one, and they are remarkable.
The one, *skiz*, along with others not mentioned, should be sought
out by travelers to the region.

Asiago (DOC): This semisoft cheese, made from partially
skimmed cow's milk, is named after the Asiago plateau in the
Vicenza Province, where it has been produced since the Middle Ages.
Asiago was originally made of sheep's milk, but cow's milk became
the standard in the seventeenth century, in keeping with the
preferences of the Veneto palate. Today, the production of the popular Asiago has spread to the entire province and to parts of
Belluno, Padua, Treviso, and Verona.

Two types of Asiago are available. One is *Asiago d'allevo*,
produced in three different stages of aging: *fresco* ("fresh,"
aged two to three months), *mezzanello* ("medium-ripe," aged three
to five months), and *vecchio* ("old," aged nine to twelve months).
An artisanal cheese still produced using traditional methods,
Asiago d'allevo is ivory in hue with a straw-colored rind and small
regular holes throughout the paste. Its consistency is compact
and uniform but tender enough to cut easily, and its flavor is agree-
able and mildly sweet. The younger stages are good melting
cheeses and respectable table cheeses. The aged cheeses are sharper
in flavor, with a more solid straw-colored paste and tan rind
that splinters when cut. They are grated and folded into polenta;
sprinkled over soups, pasta, or gnocchi; or strewn as a topping
over baked vegetables and other casserole-style dishes.

The second type of Asiago is called *pressato*. It is a bland
industrial cheese, lacking the flavor of the more traditional type.

Grana padano (DOC): One of the oldest cheeses still
made on the Italian peninsula, *grana padano* dates back to the early
part of the second millennium when the Cistercian monks of

Chiaravelle in the lower Po Valley (*padano*, "of the Po") decided to transform surplus milk into a nutritious cheese that could be stored for relatively long periods without spoiling. By the late fifteenth century, the production of *grana* had become a thriving industry, and the fame of the cheese spread throughout Italy. Today, its production in the Veneto is concentrated in the Po Valley provinces of Padua, Rovigo, Treviso, Venice, Verona, and Vicenza. *Grana* is a hard, grainy (*grana*, after its granular texture), partially skimmed cooked cow's milk cheese. It is delicate and fragrant, with an intense and complex flavor. The rind is amber colored and the interior a pale straw color.

Grana padano can be confused for Parmigiano-Reggiano, although it is not nearly as complex in flavor nor as pampered or pricey.

Montasio (DOC): The production of this distinctive cheese, named after the the mountain of its origins, began in the mid-1300s in monastic communities of the Veneto Alps. Nowadays, the area of production for *montasio* lies in the northern provinces, from Belluno to Treviso, and in parts of the Padua and Venice Provinces. This is a full-fat, semisoft cooked cow's milk cheese that is formed into wheels of about fifteen pounds each. The smooth rind is a uniform straw color; the interior is creamy hued with small, closely riddled holes. Three varieties are made: *fresco* ("fresh," aged two to three months), *semistagionato* ("partially aged," aged four to eight months), and *vecchio* (aged more than a year). The name and production dairy are branded into the rind of the cheese.

Montasio has a gentle, pleasant flavor that lasts through two years of aging. After that time, the cheese is spoiled. It is a table cheese and a grating cheese, depending on its age. In its young soft form, it is offered as an appetizer, grilled, folded into risotto, cut into matchsticks and added to salads, or grated and added to sauces for potato gnocchi (a dish I once ate in Mestre of freshly

"Medieval cheese makers invented a new cheese: Grana . . . This had an invaluable characteristic . . . it kept very well, for years even, without losing either in nutritional qualities or taste. This is why Benvenuto da Imola, about two centuries later, noted that in his times, merchants used to take a good supply [of it] on their long sea voyages."

—DOC CHEESES OF ITALY (1992)

made potato gnocchi with a sauce of radicchio and *montasio* is particularly memorable). Its best use is as a straight eating cheese with good bread and good Veneto wine.

Monte veronese (DOC): The origins of this cheese are in the isolated alpine areas of the Veneto, in the communities of the Cimbri, a group that emigrated to the area from Germany during the thirteenth century. Its area of production today, as its name implies, is the Verona Province. There are two types of *monte veronese*. One is made with whole cow's milk and aged for only thirty days; the other, called *monte veronese d'allevo*, is made of partially skimmed milk and is aged for at least three months. The rinds are thin and flexible and the interior is creamy in color. They are fragrant cheeses with a slight intensity. The longer the aging, the sharper the flavor. Both types are used as a table cheese and a grating cheese.

Provolone valpadana (DOC): Provolone is made in many parts of Italy, more commonly in the southern regions, where it originated during the Renaissance. Its production in the Veneto only began in the nineteenth century, primarily in Padua, Rovigo, Verona, and in Vicenza, where it continues to be made. It is a semisoft whole cow's milk cheese with a waxy, straw-colored rind. Its most recognizable characteristic is its wide variety of shapes, from balls to teardrops to sausages to novelty forms (piglets, for example), all in many sizes. The cheeses can be recognized by telltale strings that permit them to hang. The inner cheese is firm, smooth, and uniform in texture, and ivory in color. The flavor ranges from buttery sweet to biting sharp, depending on the method of production and length of maturation. Provolone appears in everything from antipasti to the dessert course.

Ricotta affumicata (smoked ricotta): This semisoft, pressed artisanal ricotta of sheep's milk or cow's milk is produced in the mountainous Belluno Province. *Ricotta affumicata* has a delicate but

A splinter of this sharp and ardent cheese is enough to feel the perfume of a little valley in the early morning beyond a thousand meters.

—Trevigiano writer
Giovanni Comesso

firm texture, best compared to that of feta, which makes it conducive to crumbling or shaving over pasta.

Skiz: Skiz is a lovely fresh cheese made from partially skimmed cow's milk for the express purpose of melting. It is removed from the cheese maker's kettle the moment it coagulates. If it isn't cooked in butter straight out of the kettle by the cheese maker, it is still warm when it is delivered to the local markets. It is an everyday cheese of the Veneto Alps. Like all fresh cheeses, it is essential that it be eaten on the same day it is made or at least within twenty-four hours. It is not exported (its extreme perishability prevents even air-shipping), but no one should visit the Veneto without trying it the way it is served in the Dolomites. There, in a dish called *skiz con polenta,* the cheese is sliced, sautéed on both sides in sweet butter to a beautiful golden brown, subjected to a dousing of thick, fresh cream while still hot in the pan, then served over slices of steaming-hot polenta.

Taleggio (DOC): This cheese is named after Val Taleggio, in the province of Bergamo (Lombardy), and its production is circumscribed primarily in that region, but the province of Treviso also produces it. *Taleggio* is an uncooked cheese of high breeding, a product of rich milk taken from pampered cows bred and fed carefully to ensure an exceptional eating cheese. It is made of unpasteurized or partially pasteurized whole cow's milk and formed into a distinctive rectangular shape. The soft rind is bumpy, colored ivory to blush to rust, and branded with four circles, each surrounded by a different insignia. The interior cheese is buttery, creamy colored, and highly aromatic. This is one of Italy's most delicious eating cheeses, voluptuous but classy and with a delightful velvety consistency. It is sweet and mildly nutty, with only a memory of salt, soft on the palate, and immensely luxurious.

Because *Taleggio* is an easily perishable cheese, it is important to know what to look for when buying it. The cheese should hold

The . . . growing tendency toward extending [DOC] certificates of origin should not be seen as the triumph of a questionable folklore. With this or that cheese, in fact, whole villages have expressed themselves through the centuries.

—CORRADO BARBERIS,
PRESIDENT OF THE NATIONAL
INSTITUTE OF RURAL SOCIOLOGY
(1992)

its rectangular shape well, but the crust should not be brittle, dried out, or cracked. Its interior should be characteristically creamy, not white (an indication that it is not ripe).

In the Veneto, *Taleggio* is usually eaten alone as a table cheese (the best way to taste all its virtues) with the good local red wines, or it may be brought out with fresh fruit after a meal.

Meats

Luganega or **lugana** (**juganega** in Treviso): A fresh pork sausage from the cheek and neck meat, generously flavored with aromatics. Sausage makers jealously guard their recipes for this extraordinary product.

Musetto: This is a fresh headcheese made of pork parts, flavored with salt and spices, encased, and hung for only two days.

Ossocollo: In outward appearance like a large salami, *ossocollo* is made of chopped pieces of pork from the vertebrae of the neck. After being marinated in salt and saltpeter for at least a week, the meat is massaged with a mixture of spices and pepper, rolled up, and pushed into a large sausage casing. It must hang for two months before it is ready to eat.

Prosciutto (DOC): Prosciutto has been made in the Veneto for more than two thousand years. Its production goes back to the country tradition of butchering the family pig after the harvest in preparation for preserving foods for the winter. The choice rear legs of the animal were reserved as an honored offering to the wealthy, while the less prized cuts were eaten as fresh meat or made into dried sausages and other types of *insaccati*, "encased meats," for the common people. Today, prosciutto is produced in the countryside between the Euganean Hills in the province of Padua and the Berici Hills in the province of Vicenza. Veneto prosciutto is a finely crafted ham made from pigs that are raised on buttermilk and prime cereals. These hams, formally known as *prosciutti veneti berici-euganei*, carry a DOC seal, which provides assurance of their authenticity and high quality. Their color is deep pink, their texture is buttery, their fragrance clear and sweet— likewise their delicate flavor.

Soppressa: A specialty of Treviso, *soppressa* is a type of large salami comprising 90 percent pork and 10 percent beef, flavored with salt, pepper, and various spices. It is aged for six to nine months.

Speck: There wasn't much salt in the Dolomites, where this ham originated, so hams were preserved by smoking. In the home, a net was arranged in the chimney of a fireplace, and meats and cheeses were hung there to cure. For *speck,* a fresh ham was first massaged with a mixture of salt, pepper, chopped garlic, bay, and pounded juniper berries. Each day the ham was set out in the fresh morning air to dry and massaged again every two days for a total of sixteen days. Only after this preparation was the ham hung in the chimney to smoke slowly over branches of juniper and other kinds of wood. After smoking, the ham was aged for at least six months in the cool night air to ensure that it would not dry out during this aging stage. Today, most *speck* is made in modern facilities, but some country people still smoke and age it at home. It can be thinly sliced and served like prosciutto, but the tradition is to lay a slice of it over thickly buttered black bread. Like prosciutto, speck is also used as a flavoring in the *battuto* (sautéed vegetable base) of soups, stews, and sauces.

An unsmoked variation on *speck,* massaged with a richer mixture of aromatic herbs and air-cured much like prosciutto, is made in the area as well.

Würstel: A sausage with an Austrian flavor, *würstel* is a combination of very finely minced beef and pork. It is smoked over juniper wood.

Olive Oil   Thousands of centuries ago, *l'ulivo,* the olive tree, ventured away from its mother, the Levant, and found its way to the Mediterranean.

*Sonir ulivi die curvan per il peso
dei rami/per cui le genti ci invidian di
Puglia e Sicilia.*

[In Garda] . . . the olive trees
are curved from the weight of
their branches; they are trees
which the folk of Puglia and
Sicily would envy.

—ANONYMOUS (A.D. 500)

But in its mature life, it sought the more temperate earth and
mild breezes of the north, although it still needed protection
from the cold and the insects that infected its progeny. So, in the
eighth century, the olive tree was transported to the shores of
Lake Garda in the Veneto.

For the olive tree to flourish and produce *olio*, it needs to
grow in a warm and gentle climate, with no shocks of cold or
drenching rain that might chill its roots. While most of Italy's olive
trees grow south of the Veneto, the shores of Lake Garda offer
a hospitable microclimate, a protected fecund swath where grapes
for wine and *ulivi* for superb olive oil can flourish. Even Federico
Barbarossa noted the "olivas splendidissimas" of Garda.

The excellent, delicate oil produced from the precious
northerly olive harvest has long been a prized food. While in the
rest of the Veneto, butter and, for the poor, lard figured in
every dish, Garda's cooking is based in olive oil. *Olio* was used by
wealthy households for cooking, for blessing, for preventing
ill health, and for beauty. Any excess of what was grown for home
use was valuable enough, like the good local wines, to use in
lieu of money.

Now, olive oil is a fixture in every kitchen in the Veneto,
where it has replaced the heavier butter and lard that were used
for sautéing and frying in the past.

Garda olive oils are distinguished by their intense
greenish gold color, a result of a high chlorophyll content. Their
perfume is delicately fruity and of varying strength, depending
on the precise geographic location of the mother trees, soil
drainage, and other technical variables. The flavor of these oils
has something of the sweet almond in it (in contrast to the
common Italian bitter almond). Like Umbrian oils produced from
olives that grow in the microclimate of Lake Trasimeno, Garda
oils are soft on the palate. Today, all fine extra-virgin olive

oils exported from Italy must carry government-regulated labeling indicating the region of derivation and the date of pressing, to assure the consumer that the product is genuine.

The best use of fine Garda oils is cold (that is, unheated but never refrigerated) as a condiment (exposure to flame alters the flavor of extra-virgin olive oil). The oil is also used in cooking, from sautéing to deep-frying.

Polenta

C'erano grandi campi coltivati con radici, una specie di fava e una specie di grano chiamato mahiz.

There were great fields cultivated with roots, a type of fava, and a type of grain called corn.

—Christopher Columbus, journal, November 5, 1492

Polenta e late ingrassa la culàte.

Polenta and milk fattens the rump.

—a Venetian saying

The discoveries of Christopher Columbus introduced corn in the Veneto. The Italian south was too hot and the mountain areas were too cold, but in the flatlands of the Veneto, the corn was happy. It was soon discovered that the dried kernel produced a tasty porridge, or polenta. More economical than bread and less laborious to prepare, polenta took its place, and by the 1800s, it had become a staple of the region. In the poor mountain areas, it was often the sole staple. Because the nutritional value of corn alone is minimal, pellagra and malnutrition became widespread. In the twentieth century, modern methods of food production made it possible for even the poor to supplement their polenta diets with vegetables, some meat, and other high-protein foods.

Polenta is still a favored staple in the Veneto, although now bread has taken its place to a large extent. While in the past there was only polenta, and no bread, on the table, no matter what else there was, now polenta is made depending on what is being cooked.

Cooks in the Veneto use yellow and white varieties of polenta, which are ground into a fine or coarse texture. Finely ground white polenta is preferred in the Veneto. As a general rule, the fine grind is used for porridge-style polenta; the coarse grind is more suitable for slab-style polenta that will be sliced for frying or grilling (see page 92). Cookbooks often advise using any kind of cornmeal for polenta, but this is a mistake. The type of cornmeal sold for making American-style muffins and corn bread cannot be used for polenta at all, as it produces an inedible porridge. It can be quite difficult to find Italian polenta, even in specialty shops. What is primarily imported from Italy is processed instant polenta. Some processed polentas cook too quickly and lack flavor, and are pricey as well. Others are quite good. Also readily available is already-cooked polenta that is formed into logs and vacuum-sealed, ready for slicing. It has an unpleasant flavor and no virtues except for convenience. Genuine *farina di mais*, unprocessed Italian cornmeal that produces a creamy, tasty polenta the likes of which few outside the borders of Italy have experienced, can be procured in well-stocked Italian groceries, particularly in Italian neighborhoods. This type can take up to an hour or more to cook, stirring all the while. It is no wonder that the Veneti have invented an electric polenta pot that does the stirring automatically. A happy compromise is a polenta meal that has been only partially processed to abbreviate the cooking time. Well-stocked Italian food markets carry this product, too. Look for brands that recommend cooking the polenta for less than forty minutes but more than five. Alternatively, Spanish brands of both yellow and white varieties of ground cornmeal, *harina de maiz*, sold in supermarkets, can be substituted. Both the Italian and Spanish non-instant polenta cornmeals are a fraction of the cost of the instant type and are superior in texture and flavor.

Rice   The people of Italy have been growing rice on their peninsula since ancient times, although it was not common food until the Renaissance. Today, the cultivation of rice is concentrated in a band of wetlands stretching between the Piedmont in the west and the Veneto in the east. The natural flow of water from the Po River into the plains in these regions is critical for growing it. While modern agricultural methods have made obsolete the hand labor of thousands toiling in the paddies for harvesting, the rice is unadulterated by chemical treatment or any other kind of unnatural tampering.

The Veneto's primary rice-growing area, the Bassa Veronese, is surrounded in a mist of romance. The ancient ethos of the rice farmers; the planting and harvesting rituals; the sovereignty of the rice culture (the industry is self-contained: from the sowing of seeds to its harvesting and packaging, it is all done on the plains); the pride of the rice growers; the supporting local ingredients, both wild and cultivated, for rice dishes; and the secret recipes that are not so secret—all contribute to the love affair.

Details would dispel much confusion Americans have about Italian rice varieties. Some two dozen types are grown in Italy, but primarily *arborio*, *carnaroli*, and *vialone nano* are exported. They belong to four main categories grouped according to rice shape, size, and cooking properties: common rice, which is short, round, and small-grained; semifine rice, round, pearly white grains of medium length of which *vialone nano* is an example; fine rice, a narrow grain that remains firm during cooking; and superfine rice, large, long, and tapered grains of which *arborio* and *carnaroli* are examples. The storage life of rice is about one year if it is kept in a cool, dry place. It must be stored in a sealed container to discourage infestation from the grain beetle.

Riso vialone nano veronese, commonly called *vialone nano*, is the primary rice of the Veneto and was the first rice in Italy to received the DOC mark. It is sown in 90 percent of the rice fields on the flat fertile lowlands that lie on the border that Verona shares with Mantua (Lombardy). The rice-growing area has a uniform climate, ideal growing conditions for the rice, and abundant natural springs that make it possible to cultivate rice by organic means. Venice and the provinces up to the Lake Garda area like *vialone nano*. It is considered ideal for Veneto risottos because

. . . In any of the numerous trattorie with their beautiful little signs that dot the placid little villages or in the rustic towns in the vialone nano *area, one encounters the locals passing time, crowded clandestinely in their little groups. They are elbow-to-elbow at the tables where other peaceful eaters are also intent on celebrating the virtues of the virgin grain, tasting them in various marriages [with other ingredients]. We calm ourselves with this blessed rice-earth tradition, which is so clearly manifested in the mysterious steaming platters. This is how we see this precious object of appetites.*

—GIUSEPPE RAMA,
il risotto come si fa da Isola della Scala a Castel d'Ario,
VERONA, 1996

its grain is highly absorbent and lends itself to *risotto all'onda*, "to the wave," that is, soupy, the way the seafaring Venetians like it. The mountain areas like *carnaroli*, whose grains remain distinct even when they are cooked to a creamy consistency. *Arborio* is the most widely available short-grain rice. Its high starch content makes for a creamy risotto.

Vegetables and Herbs

Many vegetables are cultivated around Venice and in the southern part of the Veneto, but a variety of wild herbs and other plants grow spontaneously alongside them in the countryside, and they, too, represent an important part of the local table. In the hills between Padua and Vicenza, wild garlic, scallions, a prized mint called *mentuccia*, mushrooms of different species, radicchio, arugula, valerian, hops, and two varieties of wild asparagus are prolific. The climate and terrain in the northern part of the Veneto provide particularly amenable growing conditions for many other wild herbs and vegetables used in cooking, including poppies, various cresses, and cumin (for its root and its seeds). Still others too numerous to mention are also prevalent in the provincial cooking.

"In Italy they sometimes broil [artichokes], and as the scaly leaves open, baste them with care extraordinary, for if a drop fall upon the coals, all is marred; that hazard escaped they eat them with juice of orange and sugar."

—JOHN EVELYN
(SEVENTEENTH CENTURY)

Artichokes *(carciofi):* Some of the most lovely vegetables of Venice are the tiny, young violet-and-green-streaked artichokes that sprout in spring, which the Venetians call *castraure* (from *castrato*, "castrated"). All lateral stems, *castraure* are cut off to be eaten as a delicacy and also to give more strength to the main plant for a later crop of mature artichokes. In lagoon gardens, particularly those of the islands of Saint Erasmus, Mazzorbo, and Mazzorbetto, ancient varieties of artichokes (among them the Chioggia, or Venice violet, of which I have already spoken) are cultivated. Their seasons are eagerly anticipated by those who are familiar with their flavor, which cannot be compared to the overgrown, tough artichokes that we face in most American markets. In April and May, the stalls of the vegetable markets throughout the region are stacked with these long-stemmed buds, which are actually the flowers of the artichoke plant. *Castraure* have a pleasantly bitter flavor that is softened by soaking them in water and lemon juice prior to cooking.

Asparagus *(asparagi):* Today, the province of Verona is one of the most important areas in Italy for the cultivation of asparagus. The area specializes in three types: the purple asparagus *(asparago viola)*, its color contrived from the practice of lengthening the harvest time, thus forcing the rhizome to acquire its brilliant mauve from prolonged exposure to the sun; the white asparagus *(asparago bianco)*; and the prized white asparagus of Cologna Veneta *(pregiato bianco di Cologna Veneta)*.

A cousin of cultivated asparagus is wild asparagus, technically asparagus chicory, a wild herb that is boiled and eaten as a vegetable dressed with extra-virgin olive oil and perhaps lemon juice, or cooked in rice dishes and various egg dishes. It makes its appearance in early spring in the lagoon area, where it is avidly picked by the locals the moment it is visible.

Hops *(luppoli* or *bruscandoli):* Hops shoots are cultivated in some parts of Europe and America for making beer, but in Italy they grow spontaneously. The Veneti call them *luppoli* or *bruscandoli*, and they are among the wild herbs that are foraged in springtime and prized for their pungent and pleasantly bitter flavor. The Euganean Hills are particularly lush with *luppoli* in season. The root and new shoots are the parts of the plant that are eaten. They are sautéed in olive oil and garlic or cooked into risottos or frittatas.

Horseradish *(cren, rafano* or *barbaforte):* The Veneti love horseradish, an Austrian influence. The flavor and sting that fresh horseradish delivers are in a different category altogether than those of bottled prepared horseradish. Fresh horseradish is widely available in American markets around the time of the Passover holiday, but it is hard to come by otherwise, outside of urban areas. For this reason, I have it growing in my garden.

Before the frost, I uproot it, cut it into manageable pieces, and freeze it for the winter and spring. It should be noted that horseradish is a useful medicine for certain ailments of the liver, is high in fiber if enough of it is eaten (I am inordinately fond of it), and is very high in vitamin C.

Lamon beans *(fagiolo di Lamon della vallata bellunese):* This bean is named after the little town of Lamon, which is nestled in the mountain province of Belluno. There it put down happy roots in the sixteenth century. These are the Veneto Alps, where the plateau that lies between Lamon and Sovramonte and the plains of Feltrina, Bellunese, and Valbelluna provide the soil and climate ideally suited to its cultivation. Another theory, expounded by a Venetian authority, Mariù Salvatori de Zuliani, is more plebeian. It traces the bean's entry into the region through the Venetian merchants who trafficked to the Americas. According to Zuliani, the farmers of Lamon were the first to plant the strange seeds. The bean pioneers suffered the ridicule of everyone around them for fooling around with the little novelty from Mexico, but soon enough, lo and behold, the sprouts were prolific and crops flourished. The Lamon bean was so tasty that soon it was in everyone's pot, from cottages perched on the highest peaks of the Veneto Alps to the villas on the Grand Canal.

Imported Lamon beans are sold in Italian specialty shops here (see page 158), and it is worth procuring them for special regional dishes. A satisfactory substitute is the pink bean, dried or canned, marketed by Spanish food companies under the Goya label and various others. I have found that canned beans sold under Italian labels are overcooked and mushy, so the Spanish companies are recommended.

There are two ways to rehydrate and cook dried beans. Whichever way, first pick over the beans and discard any stones or any beans that are discolored or damaged. For the leisurely or overnight method, put the beans in a large bowl and add cold water

to cover by three inches. Let them stand at room temperature for a minimum of six hours, or for as long as overnight. The length of soaking time will depend on the freshness of the beans: the fresher they are, the faster they will rehydrate. Drain them and rinse with cold water. Put them in a pot with cold water to cover by three inches. Bring to a boil, then reduce the heat to medium-low. Cover partially and simmer until tender but not falling apart, anywhere from thirty-five minutes to one hour, depending on the freshness of the beans. Salt the beans only after cooking, or they will become tough. I like to add about a tablespoon of salt to two cups (uncooked measure) of beans in the pot after they are cooked and permit them to soak for twenty minutes or so to absorb the salt; then drain and rinse with cold water.

For the quick method, place the picked-over beans in a pot with cold water to cover by three inches. Bring to a boil, then turn off the heat. Leave the beans in the hot water for about one hour. Drain, re-cover with water, and cook until tender. Add salt as described in the first method; drain and rinse with cold water.

Poppy *(papavero):* Throughout the Veneto, the young greens of the wild poppy *(papavero selvatico)* are eaten in winter. The blue-black seeds of the *hortense,* another poppy variety, are used in the northern region for sprinkling over pasta dishes and in baking.

Pumpkin *(zucca):* Almost everyone knows that the first pumpkins and squashes came from the New World. Over the centuries, the Italians have applied culinary art to their uses in the kitchen.

The Veneto pumpkin, *zucca,* is the most popular of all the vegetables in the region's cooking, particularly in Venice and its surroundings. Actually, two varieties are used. One is dark green and shaped somewhat like a giant acorn. The other, the Mantua *zucca,* looks more like the American butternut squash, elongated with pale yellow-green skin. Within the tough outer skin, the pumpkins are bright yellow, their flesh compact, sweet, and intensely flavored. They are unlike their namesakes commonly available in American markets, bred for Halloween jack-o'-lanterns and not suitable for cooking. The closest relative of the tasty, fleshy Italian *zucca* is the sugar pumpkin or the calabaza, the West Indian pumpkin found in many ethnic markets and, occasionally, in supermarkets. Like the *zucca*, the calabaza can grow to enormous size, thus it is always sold in pieces, kept moist under plastic wrap. These are the best substitutes for the flavor, "meaty" texture, color, and sugar content of *zucca*. The next best substitute is butternut squash, the intensely colored, thick flesh of which would be nearly equivalent except that it is several shades too sweet. Nevertheless, it will stand in beautifully for most *zucca* recipes.

Zucca is available all year in Italy, but, as an old Venetian proverb advises, the best months for eating it are August and September, when it is harvested. The only explanation that would begin to explain the Venetian passion for *zucca* is that it is one of those foods of heroic proportion, like the potato for the Irish and the corn plant for the Aztecs. These are all foods that have given sustenance when the proverbial wolf has been at the door. *Zucca* is as much a part of the fabric of the people's folklore as it is a staple of the Veneto's kitchen.

The easiest and arguably most delicious way to cook *zucca* is the way the Venetians do for *suca rostia* (roasted pumpkin, in the Venetian vernacular), a popular snack for children after school, a side dish, an appetizer, a main course, even a dessert. The habit of roasting *zucca* began centuries ago, when the squash was slipped into hot ovens while other foods were roasting. According to one's taste, it is sprinkled with salt, sugar, or nothing at all.

Radicchio: The brilliant scarlet lettuce that has become chic in recent decades is actually a member of the chicory family. There are four main types: radicchio of Verona (*veronese*), radicchio of Chioggia (*chioggiano*), variegated radicchio of Castelfranco (*variegato di Castelfranco*), and red radicchio of Treviso (*trevigiano*).

Folklore has it that before radicchio made its debut on the table, the flamboyant scarlet flower was worn as a decoration on the dresses of beautifully outfitted women attending the theater.

They are cultivated in Venice and Padua as well as in the areas that their names imply: Treviso, Chioggia, and Verona. Less known and more bitter varieties, some green, are also grown in the Veneto.

Only one type is exported to America, the Chioggia variety, which is round and compact. The other varieties, which are more esteemed by the Italians, have long heads, just like their cousin, the chicory, but the stalks are leggy and white, so much so that the *radicchi* are referred to as "broad swords" in Italy. The Treviso radicchio is deep scarlet with long, white legs extending from the base of its bulb—shaped more like a loose, oblong flower with many petals than an oversize unopened rosebud, like its Chioggia cousin. The variegated variety of Castelfranco, shaped precisely like an opened rose, is cream colored with uniform, light red–violet streaking and green tint on its outermost leaves. It can grow as large as a cabbage. Radicchio is grown on the West Coast of America now. The Chioggia, Treviso, and Castelfranco varieties are sold in farmers' markets in the San Francisco Bay Area and in some high-class supermarkets.

The notion that radicchio is for salad drives the Treviso native crazy. In its native land, its uses are endless, as is illustrated in a cookbook I came upon by Armando Zanotto, a Treviso chef. Called *Il radicchio di cucina*, it contains 617 recipes for cooking the red radicchio of Treviso and the radicchio of Castelfranco.

Valerian *(valeriana,* also *valerianella):* There are two varieties of valerian, both of which grow in the wild in springtime. At one time, valerian was found primarily in Sicily and Sardinia. Its wild seeds have spread throughout the Italian peninsula, but it is partial to the Veneto. One variety, *selene alba,* is cooked into risottos. The other, *valeriana bianca,* is used for salad. Only tender, young leaves are used in both types. Valerian is prized for its delicate and delicious flavor and also for its high vitamin and mineral content, particularly A, C, calcium, and phosphorus.

1

*salsette
e condimenti*

Sauces and Condiments

Typical rural houses near Cortina

Baccalà alla vicentina
Pastizzo autentico.
gran rarità.
real intigolo
de baccalà.

[It is] an authenic concoction
of great rarity
[this] real gravy
made from dried cod.

—a song from Vicenza,
  as quoted by Aldo Santini in
  "Friday Special: Baccalà and
  Chickpeas, a polemic on all cod
  dishes of great Venetian cuisine" (1997).

The *grande cucina veneta* once basked in sauces, which has given rise to the popular Italian epithet that the Veneti are not able to leave well enough alone. The excesses of La Serenissima are long gone, but there is still a fancy for certain embellishments. Perhaps more than anywhere else in Italy, sauces and condiments are a major part of the cooking in the Veneto. Nowhere else in Italy, for example, is salt cod *(baccalà)* transformed into a more delicate and exquisite dish than in Vicenza, home of *baccalà alla vicentina* (page 94), where a creamy sauce is an integral part of the preparation. There are also numerous *salsette,* separate little sauces, and tasty condiments that are eaten separately with fish, meat, or vegetables.

If anything can put to rest the longstanding Italian prejudice that the Veneti use sauces excessively, it would be a perusal through the fascinating and fairly recent *A tola co i nostri veci: la cucina veneziana* (roughly, *At the Table with Our Ancestors: The Venetian Kitchen*), by Mariù Salvatore de Zuliani. Only a handful of sauces are listed on their own in this cookbook, and another handful or so appear mixed in with meat and fish recipes. Between the covers is a compendium of intriguing recipes that I suspect rarely see the light of day in the contemporary Venetian home kitchen (of which, as I have said, there are sadly few), the flavors of which most Italians would find completely foreign. What I call the "foreign" aspects of Venetian cooking are due not specifically to sauces, but to the unexpected juxtaposition of flavors in certain dishes and a certain refinement in the style of cooking.

One would think that sauces and condiments would be more commonplace in Venice and the provinces close to it than in the more distant reaches of the Veneto, but while perusing a modern cookbook from Belluno, the once poor mountain region, I found at least three times as many recipes for *salsette* and condiments as Zuliani published in his masterful volume. These evidently drew from the relatively few wealthy households that existed in Belluno

Salse bele e bone,
savàia le persone!

Sauces, great and good
are the saviors of the people!

—Gianluigi Secco,
Magnar rùstego belunat

before World War II. Among the interesting collection of sauces and condiments for meat and fish were numerous variations on the horseradish theme both with and without sugar; sweet-and-sour applesauces; a condiment made from pears, apples, candied fruit, and mustard called *mostarda de la nonna* (grandmother's condiment); and a sweet-and-sour *zabaione* appropriately called *salsa bastarda* (bastard sauce).

In the best Veneto cooking, accessories such as these and others are used with a light hand, with lovely results. I think particularly of *la pearà* (page 40), the Veronese sauce based on beef marrow and bread crumbs that puts English bread sauce to shame; and the tart whortleberry sauce (in America, we can substitute blueberries and lemon) for roasted duck that I ate in Bardolino. *Salsa peverada* (page 42), a delicious, savory topping of chopped chicken livers better described as a condiment, is unique to sauces. Many of these recipes are quite versatile with meat and game; others are for fish and shellfish.

Veronese Bread Sauce

la pearà

MAKES ABOUT 4 CUPS

$^1/_4$ pound beef marrow, or $^1/_4$ cup extra-virgin olive oil

$^1/_4$ cup unsalted butter

$^1/_2$ cup fresh white bread crumbs

$3^1/_2$ cups homemade meat broth or good-quality chicken broth, brought to a boil

sea salt

freshly ground coarse black pepper

 Native to Verona, la pearà is one of the pearls of the Veneto sauce repertory. Served with bollito misto *(mixed boiled meats), it was literally my first taste of Verona. There I met up with the photographer Paolo Destefanis, and we sniffed out a good place for dinner without much effort. The* pearà *was served in a silver sauceboat that was rolled out on an elegant cart alongside a huge, handsome platter of* bollito. *The assortment of meats included capon, veal, beef, tongue, the local smoked sausage, and* nervetti *(tendon), as far as I remember.*

A simple sauce such as this one can only be as good as the ingredients of which it is comprised. It goes without saying that the marrow, butter, crumbs, and broth should be wholesome and at their freshest. The delicate extra-virgin olive oil of Lake Garda has taken the place of beef marrow in recent years.

In a medium, heavy-bottomed pot, warm the marrow or olive oil and the butter over medium-low heat until melted, stirring frequently if using marrow. Stir in the crumbs so that they absorb all of the marrow or oil and the butter. Now add the broth little by little, stirring all the while, until it is well integrated with the other ingredients. Simmer over the lowest heat, stirring frequently, until the sauce is creamy, 35 to 40 minutes. Season with salt and a generous measure of pepper. Serve hot.

Variations: There are variations of the Veronese version printed here, which include the addition of grated Parmigiano-Reggiano and minced *salumi* (cured meats). A version from Treviso, which is more peppery, is based on butter, not marrow. It may include minced local salami, hare liver, lemon juice, and a liberal amount of cinnamon and cloves.

Fresh Horseradish Sauce

cren

MAKES ABOUT 1 CUP

1 ounce stale white bread without crust
or as needed

5 ounces fresh horseradish root

$1/4$ cup white wine vinegar or as needed

pinch of sea salt

The Veneto's fiery horseradish sauce is sometimes tempered by the addition of bread, as it is here. Other versions of cren *are nothing more than horseradish and vinegar, with perhaps some parsley. Still others, such as one offered at the Osteria Penzo in Chioggia, is a mixture of* cren *and home-made mayonnaise.* Cren *is usually the sauce served with succulent* bollito misto — *the sweet, soft textures of the boiled meats and the kick of the horseradish form a mouthwatering combination. Even in the vicinity of Venice, where meat is a second thought,* bollito misto *with* cren *is a dish with a following.*

Place the bread in a medium bowl and cover with water. When it is softened, take it in your hand and squeeze out the excess water. Crumble the bread into a small bowl. Meanwhile, scrape or peel the skin off the horseradish. Grate it finely (careful, as its acid stings the eyes as much as raw onion does). Combine the bread and horseradish and, using a fork, work in as much vinegar as you will need to produce a saucelike consistency. The proportion of horseradish to bread can be adjusted according to taste. Season with salt. Serve at once.

Peverada Sauce

salsa peverada

MAKES ABOUT 1 CUP

10 fresh guinea hen or chicken livers (about 7 ounces), trimmed of fat, membranes, and any discoloration

$1/4$ cup extra-virgin olive oil

1 large clove garlic, minced

3 anchovy fillets packed in oil, finely chopped

5 ounces high-quality *soppressa* or *soppressata,* cut in thin slices and finely chopped

1 tablespoon fresh bread crumbs

3 tablespoons chopped fresh Italian parsley

Grated zest and juice of 1 large lemon

$1/3$ cup chicken broth

1 tablespoon grated *grana* or Parmigiano-Reggiano cheese

In a medium saucepan, bring 3 cups water to a boil. Slip in the livers and blanch them for 2 minutes. Drain and refresh them in cold water. Drain again and chop finely.

In an ample skillet, combine the olive oil and garlic over medium-low heat and sauté until the garlic softens, about 4 minutes. Stir in the anchovies, *soppressa,* bread crumbs, parsley, and lemon zest. Continue to sauté gently, tossing occasionally, for about 2 minutes. Now stir in the livers and sauté further until they are cooked through, about 2 minutes. Add the broth to moisten and mix in the lemon juice and cheese. There is no need for salt and pepper. Serve hot or warm.

Salsa peverada *is found throughout the Veneto wherever roasted meats are plentiful, although, according to most sources, the lovely city of Treviso, where I had my first taste of it, is its birthplace. A recipe for the sauce appears in the earliest Veneto cookbook, published in the fourteenth century. The Venetian aristocracy liked to eat it with roasted meats, hare in particular, and today it is the traditional sauce for roasted* faraona, *or guinea fowl (page 114). Peverada is a splendid sauce for roasted fowl in general, including capon, squab, turkey, or pheasant as well as for rabbit.*

Apple Condiment
for Meat and Fowl

condimento di mele per carne

MAKES ABOUT 2 CUPS

6 or 7 Golden Russet or Crispin apples

Prosecco or very dry white wine as needed

$1/4$ teaspoon sea salt

$1/4$ teaspoon freshly grated nutmeg

1 small cinnamon stick

$1/2$ teaspoon freshly ground green or pink peppercorns or a combination

5 tablespoons sugar

This recipe was kindly given by Venice-born Nicoletta Polo and, with its lovely spices, is a fitting tribute to her ancestor Marco Polo. The recipe is designed for the apples of northern Veneto, but the next best thing is the American Golden Russet or Crispin (in their harvest season), in that order. This sauce is a fine condiment for roasted pork or turkey.

Note that a food mill (passatutto)—not a food processor—will be necessary for puréeing, as the apple skins remain during cooking to add flavor and vitamins. Only the mill will permit you to purée while leaving the skins behind.

Core the apples, but leave them whole with their skins intact. Pack them into a heavy saucepan in which they fit snugly. Pour the wine into the pan to reach halfway up the sides of the apples. Then pour in water to cover the apples. Add the salt, nutmeg, cinnamon, peppercorns, and sugar. Bring to a boil over high heat and immediately reduce the heat to medium. Simmer, uncovered, until most of the liquid is evaporated and the skins slip off the apples by themselves, about 1 hour. The flesh should give way easily to the prod of a knife or fork. If there is too much liquid, continue to simmer until most of it evaporates. Remove from the heat and permit the apples to cool. Fish out the cinnamon stick and discard.

Fit a food mill with a large-holed disk attachment. Position the mill over a sturdy bowl of a size that will allow you to rest the bottom clamps of the mill over the bowl while you pass the apples through it, cranking the handle steadily to purée. If there is any liquid, pass it through the mill with the apples. Be sure to press down on the handle when the pulp remains in the food mill to extract as much flavor from the peels as possible. Taste and add sugar if necessary. The sauce should be sweet, but not excessively so. Serve at room temperature. The sauce can be stored, tightly covered, in the refrigerator, for up to 5 days.

Appetizers and Snacks

Venetian Carnival puppets

*Our dogs, Texas (a Greyhound)
and Bubba (a Vizsla), aside from being
"stars" on the* vaporetto, *are pretty
popular in a bunch of bars and restaurants in Venice.*

*And they are very knowledgeable (about
food and drink, especially).*

*They know lots of secrets—for example:
Do you know what Venetians call
a single glass of wine? It's an* ombra,
which means a shadow, in Italian.

Why?

*Well, during the nineteenth century,
the gentle folk of Venice,* la gente
Veneziana, *taking their afternoon sip
of wine, amid good conversation
at tables on Piazza San Marco, were
shaded from the sun by the shadow of
canopies attached to the bell tower.
And so, a glass of wine is a shadow—
an* ombra.

—Peter Wexler,
*The Remarkable Adventures of Texas
& Bubba in Venice*

The appetizer course is taken seriously in Venice, where it may be eaten at any time. The tradition is no doubt a reflection of the very ornateness of Venice, transmitted to the table. Crisp and puffy deep-fried pumpkin flowers may arrive before dinner in a golden pile (for a main course, they might be stuffed with cheese). Or the young radicchio flower may be batter-fried for a flamboyant teaser. The very notion of going a bit beyond the ordinary or of creating pleasure beyond what is expected in the normal course of a meal is entirely Venetian.

The most engaging of all Venetian appetizers, *cicheti*, are of humble origins. *Cicheto* derives from the vernacular of the neighboring Piedmont, where *cichetare* means "to drink," but only in little sips or a small quantity (while *cichetone*, the superlative, describes someone who eats too much). *Cicheti* can be anything from tidbits of cheese and boiled eggs to crispy deep-fried savories of seafood or vegetables.

Cicheti were once poor foods, finger foods eaten standing up at a counter in casual bars that workers could duck into for a nibble and a slug and some noisy camaraderie. Places where *cicheti* are found are still casual, frequented by locals, and, more often than not, out of the way. Considering the pedestrian nature of the city, the old ritual of *andare a cicheto*, "going for a nibble," is not surprising. When the lunch or dinner hour is still a long way off and the restaurants are closed, or before boarding the crowded ferries for home in other parts of the lagoon, Venetians queue up at the counters of the *cicheti* bars. In the evening, going for *cicheti* supposes also *andare per l'ombra*, "getting into the shade," for an *ombra*, a glass of wine or Prosecco—or perhaps a shot of local *grappa*.

The cities in the mainland provinces also tend toward courses to whet the appetite. In the countryside, the antipasti offered are usually simpler—a sampling of locally cured meats, perhaps, but no matter what, a pool of creamy, hot polenta is passed along with the platter.

Eggs Scrambled
with Sage Extract

salviata

FOR 4 PEOPLE

$1/4$ cup packed fresh sage leaves,
finely minced

3 tablespoons boiling water

7 eggs

3 tablespoons freshly grated Parmigiano-
Reggiano cheese

$1/2$ teaspoon sea salt

2 tablespoons unsalted butter

 *This is based on a very old recipe of the Veneto
and is simple enough. Fresh sage leaves are
pounded or minced to render an extract that is
used to flavor scrambled eggs. The combination
of eggs and sage is very pleasing. Eggs are
not eaten for breakfast in Italy but rather as
antipasti or* merende *(mid-afternoon) snacks.
This, in Venice, is a* cicheto.

In a teacup, combine the sage and boiling water and let
steep for about 30 minutes. Transfer the mixture to
a blender. Blend on high speed for about 15 seconds. Pass
the liquid through a strainer lined with cheesecloth
or a paper towel. Squeeze the cloth to extract as much juice
as you can. Measure out 2 teaspoons of the sage extract
to add to the eggs.

In a medium bowl, lightly beat together the eggs, cheese,
salt, and the 2 teaspoons sage extract.

In an ample skillet, warm the butter over medium heat
until it is melted and hot but not brown. Immediately pour
the egg mixture into the pan. With a wooden spoon, begin
to mix the eggs after they have just set, as for scrambled
eggs; continue to mix the eggs until they are evenly and
lightly cooked. Take care not to overcook them.

Turn the eggs out immediately onto a warmed plate and
serve at once.

Stuffed Crab

granceola alla veneziana

FOR 2 PEOPLE

1 live male crab and 1 live female crab to yield 1$^1/_2$ pounds crabmeat

$^1/_4$ cup extra-virgin olive oil

juice of 1 lemon

1 small clove garlic, minced (optional)

sea salt

freshly ground white or black pepper

1 tablespoon chopped fresh Italian parsley

Granceola alla veneziana, *stuffed spider crab, is one of Venice's most famous seafood dishes. The meaty, tasty spider crab, native to the Mediterranean, the Adriatic, the North Sea, and the eastern Atlantic, is spiny and hard-shelled and has eight legs and two claws. The whole crabs are cooked, and their meat is extracted, chopped, flavored (garlic may be included), and replaced in the empty shell in a tantalizing mound. In Venice, equal quantities of male and female spider crabs are used because the flesh of the male crab is tastier, but the female is meatier. Other kinds of crabs can also be used. Keep in mind that after cooking, they should yield 1 ½ pounds of meat.*

If live crabs are not easy to come by, substitute freshly cooked crabmeat (it can be special-ordered from some fishmongers) and serve the seasoned crabmeat in cocktail cups or large scallop shells.

Fill a kettle with enough water to cover the crabs and bring the water to a rapid boil. It is instant and thus more humane to kill the crabs by severing their spinal cords than by boiling them to death. To sever their cords, plunge a large, sharp knife between their eyes, making a single quick, deep incision in each, then slip them into the boiling water. Cook over high heat for exactly 7 minutes, then drain immediately.

When the crabs are cool enough to handle but are still warm, twist off the claws and legs. With a lobster cracker, meat mallet, or nutcracker, crack the claws all over. Keep the shell intact if you are using it as a receptacle for the crabmeat later. With the aid of a lobster pick, pick out the meat from the claws and legs, discarding any cartilage, and place the meat in a bowl. Then, with your fingers, pull off the "apron" on the underside of each crab body and discard it. Holding the body in both hands, slip your thumb under the shell where the apron was connected, and pull the top shell from the body. Use a spoon to remove any coral and the grayish green liver from the top shell and, if desired, place it in the bowl with the crabmeat. Remove and discard the spongy gills. With a lobster pick, extract the meat inside the shell and add to the bowl. Rinse off the shells, if using, and set them aside.

Using a fork, flake the meat and break up the coral and liver, if using. If using lump crabmeat, pick it over and remove any shell fragments that may remain, then flake the meat with a fork. Season with the olive oil, lemon juice, garlic (if using), salt, and pepper. Gently stir in the parsley. Spoon the crabmeat mixture back into the shells or into cocktail cups and serve.

Steamed Mussels with Ginger and Lemongrass

cozze con zenzero e citronella

FOR 4 PEOPLE

4 pounds not-too-large mussels

1 stalk lemongrass

6 tablespoons extra-virgin olive oil

5 large cloves garlic, minced

4 slices fresh ginger, each about 1 inch in diameter and $1/8$ inch thick

1 cup dry white wine

sea salt

freshly ground white pepper

Another one of Corte Sconta's simple and delicious seafood appetizers, flavored with citronella, a type of lemongrass. Be sure to buy mussels with tightly closed shells or ones that close tightly when touched. Most mussels are now farmed and are free of sand, barnacles, and even beards. With these mussels, there is no need for the kind of meticulous cleaning necessary for wild mussels.

With a very stiff brush, scrub the mussels well. Pull or cut off any beards. Use a small, sharp knife to scrape off any barnacles. Rinse well with cold water to remove any traces of sand. Place the mussels in a large bowl with cold water to cover and let stand for 1 to 3 hours to cleanse them of any sand. Drain and rinse again, discarding any mussels whose shells do not close tightly to the touch.

Strip away the tough outer leaves of the lemongrass and cut off any dried-out parts. Cut the stalk into 3 equal pieces.

In a heavy Dutch oven large enough to accommodate the mussels easily, warm the olive oil, garlic, and ginger over medium-low heat. Sauté until the garlic is soft, 2 to 3 minutes. Add the mussels and lemongrass and, using a wooden spoon, toss them in the pan to coat them with the oil mixture. Pour in the wine. Cover the Dutch oven tightly, raise the heat to medium-high, and bring to a boil. Reduce the heat to medium and simmer until the mussels are fully open, 2 to 3 minutes. Remove from the heat and taste for salt; add pepper to taste.

Discard any mussels that failed to open; fish out the lemongrass and discard. Using a slotted spoon, divide the mussels evenly among shallow bowls. Use a large spoon or ladle to spoon the broth from the pan over each mound of mussels.

Turkey Meatballs with Citrus and Ginger Sauce

*polpette di tacchino agli agrumi
con lo zenzero*

FOR 4 PEOPLE

FOR THE MEATBALLS:

1 ounce stale white bread without crust, soaked in milk or poultry stock until softened

1 pound ground turkey

2 bunches green onions, including 3 inches of green tops, finely chopped

1 clove garlic, minced

1 egg, lightly beaten

$1/2$ teaspoon sea salt

freshly ground white or black pepper

olive oil for deep-frying

$1/2$ cup unbleached flour

FOR THE SAUCE:

2-inch piece fresh ginger, peeled and grated

grated zest and juice of 1 navel orange

juice of 1 lemon

1 tablespoon finely chopped lemongrass

sea salt

freshly ground white pepper

 The Venetians are fond of meatballs, made either from chopped leftover cooked meats bound with egg and herbs or from ground raw meats that may include veal, beef, pork, or turkey. Polpette di carne are moistened with everything from sweet-and-sour dressings to the universal tomato sauce

To make the meatballs: Wring the bread dry and place it in a large bowl with the turkey, green onions, garlic, egg, salt, and pepper to taste. Mix together to distribute the ingredients evenly. Fry a small nugget of the mixture in a little olive oil, then taste and adjust the seasoning of the mixture. Form the mixture into walnut-sized balls.

Spread the flour on a sheet of waxed paper. In a deep skillet, pour in the olive oil to a depth of 2 inches and heat over medium-high heat until it is hot enough to cause the meat to sizzle up on contact. Line a platter with paper towels.

Dredge the meatballs in the flour, shaking off the excess, and slip them into the hot oil. Do not dredge the meatballs until the moment you are ready to fry them or the flour coating will become too damp to form a crisp coating in the oil. Fry evenly, turning as needed, until the meatballs are cooked through and nicely browned, about 8 minutes. Using a wire skimmer or tongs, transfer the meatballs to the paper towels to drain, shaking off any excess oil as you lift them out of the pan.

To make the sauce: Combine all the ingredients, including salt and pepper to taste, and mix well. Serve the meatballs warm or at room temperature. Use the sauce for dipping.

Carpaccio of Venison on a Bed of Salad Greens, Apple Matchsticks, and Walnuts

carpaccio di capriolo su letto di insalata, mele a fiammifero, e noci

FOR 4 PEOPLE

$1/2$ cup plus $1/3$ cup extra-virgin olive oil

3 tablespoons high-quality balsamic vinegar

juice of $1/2$ lemon

$1/2$ teaspoon Dijon mustard

1 anchovy fillet packed in olive oil, finely chopped

sea salt

freshly ground black pepper

1 pound organic young venison fillet, partially frozen

about 8 ounces mixed baby salad greens

1 large tart green apple

8 walnut halves, chopped

Paolo Destefanis sent me this recipe after returning from one of his photo missions in the Dolomites. It is a specialty of Il Capriolo in Vodo di Cadore, in the mountainous Belluno Province, where venison is a favorite. The fillet or loin skirt of young venison is used for this dish, and it should be partially frozen before cutting in order to slice it paper-thin. While vension is uncommon in American markets, it is farm-raised for restaurants and can be purchased by mail-order from purveyors of specialty meats (see page 158). Capriolo, roe deer, is found in Italy. It is a true delicacy, for which young venison can be substituted. Venison is a meat Americans should love. It has little fat, and what there is of it is primarily mono- or polyunsaturated. Do not be surprised by the use of balsamic vinegar here. While it originates in Modena (Emilia-Romagna), it is now widely used as a condiment in central and northern Italy.

In a shallow bowl or small glass baking dish large enough to accommodate the meat later, combine the ½ cup olive oil, 2 tablespoons of the balsamic vinegar, the lemon juice, mustard, anchovy, and salt and pepper to taste. Stir to mix well. Using a sharp knife, cut the meat against the grain into paper-thin slices. Add the meat to the marinade, toss to coat evenly, and store in the refrigerator for 6 to 8 hours.

When ready to serve, arrange a bed of greens on each of 4 salad plates. Core and peel the apple, then cut it into *fiammiferi* (matchsticks); distribute the apple pieces evenly over the greens on each plate. Remove the venison from the refrigerator and lift the slices out of the marinade; discard the marinade. Arrange the slices in a fan pattern over the apple pieces on each plate. Distribute the walnuts evenly over the top of each serving. Prepare a dressing with the remaining ⅓ cup olive oil and 1 tablespoon balsamic vinegar, and season to taste with salt and pepper. Drizzle the dressing evenly over the venison slices and salad greens. Serve immediately.

Savory Pumpkin Pie

torta salata di zucca

FOR 8 PEOPLE

FOR THE PASTRY DOUGH:

2 cups unbleached flour

1 teaspoon sea salt

2 teaspoons chopped fresh sage
or 1 teaspoon crumbled dried sage

1 teaspoon crumbled dried rosemary

7 tablespoons unsalted butter

$^1/_3$ cup ice water

FOR THE FILLING:

1 small sugar pumpkin, butternut squash,
or calabaza (about 3 pounds)

1 tablespoon unsalted butter
at room temperature

2 ounces *speck* or pancetta,
chopped and sautéed until cooked, but soft

1 cup freshly grated Parmigiano-Reggiano
cheese

$^1/_4$ cup freshly grated pecorino romano
cheese

1 cup shredded Gruyère cheese

1 extra-large egg

1 teaspoon sea salt

pinch of freshly ground black pepper

 An unusual pumpkin pie for American tastes, this torta di zucca *is savory rather than sweet. It is baked in a pie dish, and when set, small wedges can be cut for appetizer portions or for serving as a* cicheto *with an* ombra *of red wine. This recipe was kindly given to me by Camilla Destefanis, a good home cook.*

Because the pastry dough calls for a generous amount of butter, it may be easier to work with if made a day in advance and chilled.

To make the pastry dough: In a medium bowl, combine the flour, salt, sage, and rosemary and stir to mix. Add the butter and, using a pastry blender, cut it in until the mixture resembles pealike pieces. Sprinkle in the ice water and, using a fork, stir and toss the mixture until it comes together in a rough mass. If necessary, use a little more ice water to moisten the dough enough for it to form a unified dough. Work quickly in order to prevent the butter from warming too much, which would prevent a flaky crumb from forming. (The dough can be made successfully in a food processor using the metal blade.) Divide the dough into 2 portions, with 1 portion twice as large as the other. Cover each portion with plastic wrap and chill for a minimum of 1 hour.

To make the filling: While the dough is chilling, preheat the oven to 400 degrees F. Line a baking sheet with aluminum foil and oil the foil. Cut the squash in half lengthwise and scrape out and discard the seeds. Place the squash halves, cut side down, on the prepared baking sheet. Bake until tender throughout, about 40 minutes. Test for doneness with a sharp knife or thin skewer; it should meet no resistance. Remove the squash from the oven and reduce the temperature to 350 degrees F.

When the squash is cool enough to handle, peel off the skin. Mash the pulp well with a fork or potato masher in a bowl or purée it in a food processor and transfer to a bowl. Add the butter, *speck*, cheeses, egg, salt, and pepper and mix well.

Select a 10-inch glass or ceramic pie dish or a 9-inch pie dish for a deeper filling. Butter and flour the pie dish and shake out the excess flour. Remove the larger dough portion from the refrigerator. On a lightly floured work surface, roll out the dough into a round at least 2 inches larger in diameter than the pie dish and about ⅛ inch thick. Carefully transfer the round to the prepared pie dish and ease it into the bottom and sides. Trim the edges to leave an overhang of about ½ inch that can be crimped later to form an attractive edge. Remove the remaining dough from the refrigerator and roll it out in the same manner into a round at least as large as the diameter of the pan and about ⅛ inch thick. Using a fluted pastry wheel, cut the round into strips about ½ inch wide. Pour the filling into the pastry-lined dish. Using the pastry strips, weave a lattice crust over the filling. Then fold the overhang of the bottom crust inward and crimp as for a fruit pie.

Slide the pie into the oven and bake until a skewer passed into the center of the filling comes out clean and the crust is golden, 55 to 60 minutes. Transfer to a rack to cool. Serve warm or at room temperature, cut into small wedges.

3

primi

First Courses of Soup, Pasta, and Rice

Grocery store in Bardolino

Like so many traditional dishes, cazunzièi are minivignettes of history. The influence of the Austro-Hungarian Empire is evident: butter and beet in the filling, butter and poppy seeds on top.

When in other lands and situations you might encounter an anonymous plate of rice, the memory will have a sudden flash of how differently Verona and Mantua use this food, which constitutes more than half of a day's ration of food for a billion and a half people around the world.

—Giuseppe Rama,
Il risotto come si fa da Isola della Scala a Castel d'Ario

A dish of soup, pasta, or risotto is considered a first course on the Venetian table, as it is elsewhere in Italy. The second course of meat or fish follows, which may or may not be served with polenta.

In the past, the soups served as *primi* were thick, substantial creations, one-pot meals based on vegetables, beans, barley, or rice, perhaps fortified with a little meat or cheese. They were flavorful restoratives for a life of work and hardship. In modern times, a lighter style of soup has grown out of these hearty bowls, but beans are still a favorite soup ingredient throughout the Veneto.

If the Veneto has any pasta to call its own, they are *bigoli*, thick noodles. Most popular of all are *bigoli* tossed in a hot skillet with a sauce of olive oil, anchovies, and onions.

Cazunzièi, the Veneto's version of ravioli, go by many spellings and pronunciations and are prepared in at least as many ways. They are stuffed with various fillings including beet, pumpkin, or *gamaite*, wild greens that are close in flavor to spinach. There is a pleasantly pink version with a beet-and-potato stuffing from the Ampezzo, in northern Belluno. In other parts of the province, *cazunzièi* are stuffed with pumpkin or spinach, or with ham perfumed with cinnamon, then topped with melted butter and grated smoked ricotta.

Potato gnocchi are everywhere in the mainland region, moistened with the *salsa di pomodoro* that is now universally Italian, and also sauced in ways that are unique to the Veneto. In the Cadore zone of the Belluno Province, *gnocchi alla cadorina* are flavored with melted butter and the local smoked ricotta; in Treviso they are made with, or topped with, a radicchio sauce. In general they are paired with butter and sage, butter and cinnamon or nutmeg, artisanal cheeses, or sauces of seasonal ingredients such as wild game, wild mushrooms, or greens and herbs.

It is hard to say whether gnocchi are indigenous to the Veneto, but they have been its most important form of pasta since the introduction of the potato in the 1800s. Everyone had access to potatoes, even the very poor, and gnocchi became widespread. But the history of gnocchi in the Veneto dates to before the arrival of the potato. In 1406, a terrible famine struck Verona, causing the city's ruling family, the Scaligeri, to submit to the domination of La Serenissima. In recognition of the event, the Venetian Republic instituted a festival of abundance, distributing food, including gnocchi, throughout the city. The gnocchi of those times were formed of flour, butter, and grated cheese.

But of all of the Veneto's first courses, rice is unsurpassed. Nowhere else in Italy is risotto cooked with such enthusiasm and imagination. The Veneto's risottos are intensely flavored with the likes of wild herbs, poppy greens, cresses, hops, and wild asparagus. The incomparable sugary peas of early spring make their debut in Venice's favorite rice dish, *risi e bisi*, and when the bittersweet flower of all lettuces, radicchio, blooms, risotto becomes tinged with its scarlet hue. The Venetians consider risotto made with the celebrated pumpkins of Chioggia to be one of its most important dishes. Venice also loves risottos of seafood, while the provinces stir up land-based versions. The region's fine wines are not only for drinking, but also for stirring into risottos, as in the *risotto al Bardolino* and *risotto al prosecco.*

It is essential to know what types of rice to use in making the local specialties. For a proper risotto, the only rices that are suitable are those that are cultivated in the Po tributaries: *vialone nano, carnaroli,* and *arborio* (page 28).

Since 1406, a gnocchi festival has been celebrated every year on Venerdì Gnoccolare, Verona's version of Mardi Gras. The celebration is on a grand scale, the most flamboyant of all food festivals in the Veneto. The tradition begins with the election of the papà del gnoco, *who runs for election each year in the city of Verona. A candidate with any hopes for bearing the gnocchi scepter must be old and* robusto, *with flowing white hair and beard and rosy cheeks—una persona simpatica— and small enough to ride comfortably on the ceremonial steed, a donkey. The* papà del gnoco *leads the Verona carnival holding a scepter—a long fork— on which gnocchi are impaled. Like other royals, he spends his time attending ceremonial civic functions, visiting schools and sick children in hospitals, and going around doing general good works.*

Red Bean and Barley Soup
from Pagnano

minestra di orzo e fasoi

FOR 4 TO 6 PEOPLE

8 ounces (about $1^{1}/_{8}$ cups) dried Lamon, *borlotti,* or pink beans, or 1 can (16 ounces) pink beans

1 large meaty ham bone, excess fat removed, or 2 quarts (8 cups) homemade meat broth or good-quality chicken broth

$2^{1}/_{2}$ cups water

6 tablespoons extra-virgin olive oil

6 ounces tasty smoked ham, cubed, if not using ham bone

2 onions, chopped

2 carrots, peeled and chopped

2 celery stalks, including leaves, chopped

2 large cloves garlic, chopped

2 bay leaves or 4 to 6 large sage leaves

$^{1}/_{2}$ cup pearl barley (see Note), soaked and cooked according to package instructions

2 teaspoons sea salt

freshly ground coarse black pepper

 Barley was a staple many centuries before pasta was established anywhere in Italy. This is a classic dish of the Treviso area that predates the ubiquitous pasta e fagioli, *pasta and beans (fasoi is local dialect for* fagioli*). I had a pleasant rendition of it in a rustic trattoria in the small town of Pagnano, near Castelfranco.*

Note that salt is added only after the soup is fully cooked. This ensures that the beans remain tender during cooking.

If using dried beans, rehydrate by the overnight method or quick method and cook them as directed on page 32; drain and set aside. If using canned beans, drain and set aside.

If using a ham bone, place it in an ample pot with water to cover (about 2½ cups) and bring to a boil; reduce the heat to a lazy simmer and cook, partially covered, until a tasty broth is formed. This should take about 50 minutes. Remove the bone from the broth and skim the fat from the surface. You should have about 8 cups of broth. Using a knife, cut all the meat from the bone into bite-size pieces and set it aside for adding to the soup at the last minute. Set the broth aside as well. If using the meat broth, reserve.

In a Dutch oven or wide, deep skillet, warm the olive oil over medium heat. If not using a ham bone, add the smoked ham pieces and sauté to color the ham, about 5 minutes. Using a slotted spoon, transfer the ham to a bowl and set it aside for adding to the soup at the last minute. Pour any olive oil that has accumulated in the bowl with the ham back into the pan.

Now add the onions, carrots, celery, garlic, and bay leaves to the Dutch oven and sauté over medium-low heat until the vegetables are very soft but not at all browned, 12 to 15 minutes. A lid can be placed askew over the pan to encourage the vegetable mixture to soften nicely as it sautés gently.

Meanwhile, roughly crush the beans with a potato masher or a fork. Then, when the vegetables are nicely softened, add the beans to the pan. Stir in all but 1 cup of the broth. Cover and simmer over medium-low heat, stirring often to prevent sticking, until the beans are thoroughly softened and nearly disintegrated, 30 to 45 minutes; the timing depends on how long it takes to soften the skins of the beans thoroughly.

Remove from the heat and pass the soup through a food mill to form a smooth purée. If a food mill is not available, the soup may be puréed in a food processor, but the texture will be grainier.

Return the purée to the Dutch oven over medium-low heat; stir in the remaining 1 cup broth until a creamy but not dense consistency is formed. Then add the cooked barley and ham pieces and heat through. Add the salt and plenty of pepper. Serve the soup steaming hot.

Note: Medium pearl barley, the variety found in most American markets, has been processed to reduce its cooking time. The method removes some of its nutrients as well. Whole barley, found in health-food stores, is more nutritious, but it takes far longer to cook.

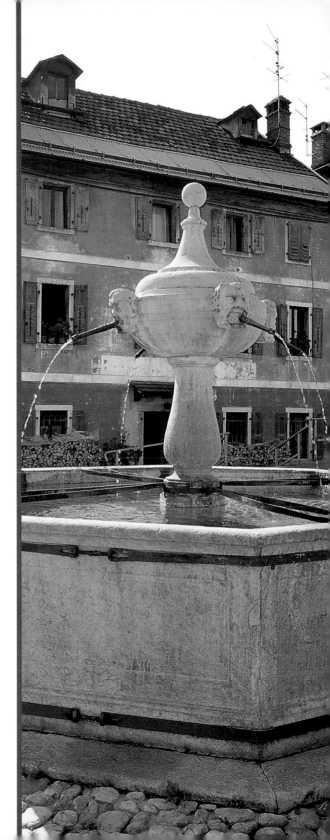

Pasta and Beans

pasta e fasioi

FOR 6 PEOPLE

5 cups drained cooked Lamon beans
(see recipe introduction)

6 tablespoons extra-virgin olive oil

1 onion, chopped

2 carrots, peeled and chopped

1 celery stalk, including leaves, chopped

2 bay leaves

2 teaspoons fresh rosemary leaves, minced,
or 1 teaspoon crumbled dried rosemary

1 potato, peeled and cut into small dice

8 ounces ham, cut into small dice

4 ounces fresh or imported Italian dried
pappardelle

1 teaspoon kosher salt

sea salt

$1/2$ teaspoon freshly ground black pepper

This is the classic pasta e fasioi (fasioi is the local dialect for fagioli, "beans") of Belluno, where the fat and tasty Lamon beans grow. Pink beans, either dried, rehydrated, and cooked (page 32) or canned, will have to do where Lamon beans cannot be procured. Pasta and bean combinations in the south of Italy typically include dried macaroni-type pasta, but this is not so in the Veneto. Pappardelle, wide egg noodles, are made by hand specifically for the soup, giving it a refined character. If this is not practical, you may substitute high-quality dried pappardelle. The traditional method for making the soup is to make a broth with a large, meaty ham bone or from pieces of salted pork. The meat is taken off the bone (or the cured pork is diced), and added to the beans. American cooks who find procuring a ham bone impractical may substitute a large, thick slice of ham.

Rinse the cooked beans well in cold water, then drain. Set them aside.

In a deep, wide pot, warm the olive oil over low heat. Add the onion, carrots, celery, bay leaves, and rosemary, cover partially, and cook, stirring occasionally, until the mixture is nicely softened, about 8 minutes. Stir in the potato, ham, and beans and continue to cook to combine the flavors, about 5 minutes. Pour in 7 cups of water and bring to a boil. Reduce to a simmer and cook gently, partially covered, until the potatoes are cooked through, about 35 minutes. The idea is to simmer the soup gently at this point to develop its flavor.

In the meantime, fill a separate pot with 2 quarts of water and bring to a rolling boil. Stir in the *pappardelle* and kosher salt. Cook the pasta only briefly, until al dente, about 1 minute if fresh, 2 minutes if dried. Drain, then rinse the pasta with cold water. Stir the pasta into the soup and season with sea salt to taste and the pepper. Serve immediately.

Wine Soup

sugoli

FOR 2 OR 3 PEOPLE

4 cups full-bodied dry red wine

$1/2$ cup sultanas

$1/4$ cup unbleached flour

$1/4$ cup sugar

grated zest of 1 lemon

$1/4$ cup pine nuts, lightly toasted

1 cinnamon stick

3 whole cloves

The preparation of this beguiling soup, made from the mosto *(must, or pulp) that remains of the black grapes after they are pressed for wine, is an ancient tradition of the wine-producing areas of the Veneto (the words* sugoli *and* sugolo *are likewise ancient local dialect). Red wine can be substituted for the must and produces a perfectly lovely soup, one which I have no doubt will find a following in America.*

In a small saucepan, combine the wine and sultanas and bring to a boil. Remove from the heat and permit to soak for at least 1 hour to plump the raisins fully. Strain the raisins, reserving the wine. Measure out 1 cup of the wine. Little by little, blend the flour into the cup of wine, using a wooden spoon to mix well and smooth out any lumps. It is always a good idea to pass the wine-and-flour paste through a sieve to remove any lumps.

In a medium saucepan, bring the remaining wine to a boil with the sugar and lemon zest, stirring to dissolve the sugar. Slowly stir in the wine-and-flour mixture, using a wooden spoon to blend well. Add the pine nuts, raisins, cinnamon, and cloves and simmer for 10 minutes to blend the flavors. Taste and add up to 2 tablespoons sugar if necessary. The amount of sugar needed will depend on the dryness of the wine and how its flavors are altered during cooking.

Remove from the heat and permit to cool to room temperature. Discard the cinnamon stick and cloves. Serve at room temperature or chilled.

Pumpkin Soup

passato di zucca

FOR 6 TO 8 PEOPLE

1 small sugar pumpkin, calabaza,
or butternut squash ($2^1/_2$ to 3 pounds)

4 tablespoons ($^1/_2$ stick) unsalted butter

1 tablespoon olive oil

2 onions, grated or finely chopped

8 thin slices fresh ginger, each about
2 inches in length, peeled

8 cups milk

1 teaspoon sea salt

freshly ground white pepper

fresh mint leaves, torn into small pieces
(optional)

The pumpkin soup of Venice is a simple affair of puréed pumpkin cooked with milk. Be sure to use sugar or West Indian (calabaza) pumpkin; American pumpkins produced for jack-o-lanterns are neither fleshy nor flavorful enough to stand on their own. Butternut squash is the next best substitute for the various varieties of zucca the Venetians use for this soup. Sautéed onion and fresh ginger add a great deal of flavor.

Preheat the oven to 400 degrees F. Line a baking sheet with aluminum foil and oil the foil. Cut the squash in half lengthwise and scrape out and discard the seeds. Place the squash halves, cut side down, on the prepared baking sheet. Bake until tender throughout, about 40 minutes. Test for doneness with a sharp knife or thin skewer; it should meet no resistance. Remove from the oven and, when cool enough to handle, peel off the skin and cut the squash into small dice.

In a soup pot, melt the butter with the olive oil over medium-low heat. Add the onions and sauté very gently until thoroughly softened but not at all browned, 10 to 12 minutes. Add the diced squash and the ginger and sauté to marry the flavors, about 5 minutes. Now stir in 3 cups of the milk and cook over low heat until the mixture begins to simmer. Remove the pot from the heat and allow the mixture to cool somewhat. Then pass the mixture through a food mill or purée in a blender or food processor.

Return the purée to the pot, stir in the remaining 5 cups milk, and simmer for about 12 more minutes to thicken. Add more milk if the consistency is too thick (it should be thick enough to coat the spoon) and heat through. Season with the salt and pepper.

Ladle into warmed bowls, strew the mint on the surface, if using, and serve at once.

Potato Gnocchi

gnocchi di patate

FOR 4 PEOPLE

2 pounds boiling potatoes of uniform size

1³/₄ cups unbleached flour or as needed

1 teaspoon sea salt

2 tablespoons kosher salt

Pastissada (page 97)

 In the Veneto, the sauce made for gnocchi might be as simple as melted butter and grated smoked ricotta, known as puina, *or it might be made of radicchio and cream, like one I ate in Mestre. The most famous of all gnocchi and sauce combinations is that of Verona, where the tender dumplings are dressed with* pastissada, *a dish emblematic of Venerdì Gnoccolare, the Verona carnival.*

The potatoes of the Veneto are grown in the Cadore part of the Dolomites. Their flesh is dry and intensely flavorful, the perfect consistency for proper gnocchi. The general principle for making light gnocchi is to introduce as little moisture into the dough as possible, thus preventing the absorption of too much flour by the potatoes. I bake rather than boil the potatoes to eliminate as much water as I can. The best device for mashing the cooked potatoes to a lump-free consistency is a potato ricer, which can be bought in cookware shops.

Preheat the oven to 400 degrees F. Scrub the potatoes, dry them, and place them on a baking sheet. Bake until tender, passing a skewer or sharp knife through the center to test, about 40 minutes. Remove from the oven and let them cool just until they can be handled, then peel them.

Turn the flour out onto a work surface and add the sea salt. Make a well in the center. Pass the potatoes through a potato ricer held over the well. Using a fork, incorporate the potatoes into the flour, drawing the flour in as you work the mass into dough. The amount of flour that will be absorbed is not predictable, but to ensure light gnocchi, work in as little flour as possible to make a workable dough. You may need a little less or more than is called for here, so work it into the potatoes gradually. Knead the dough for 5 minutes once it is formed. Divide it into quarters and refrigerate the sections you are not immediately working with until you are ready to use them. (Do not refrigerate for too long or you will have an unworkable dough.)

With your hands, form a section of dough into a long rope about ³/₄ inch in diameter. With a knife, cut the rope into sections of the same width, about ³/₄ inch. Use the side of a box grater or the tines of a fork to shape the pieces. If using the grater, take each little piece you've cut and, holding it between your thumb and forefinger, roll it along the side with the large holes, pushing your thumb into the dough as you do so. If using a fork, press the piece of dough along the tines to form the gnocchi. A concave dumpling should result. You can also push the little pieces of dough against the floured work surface, using your thumb to push a hollow in the center. The concave shape allows the gnocchi to cook uniformly rather than remain doughy in the center. Don't worry if the dough is a little sticky as you work with it; simply dust the grater or fork with flour. (If it is too sticky, you probably need to incorporate a little more flour into the dough.)

In a large pot, bring about 5½ quarts of water to a rapid boil and add the kosher salt. While the water is heating, position a slotted spoon and perforated broiler tray or colander next to the stove. Choose a large, shallow, oven-proof serving dish in which to transfer the gnocchi once they are drained. Smear the dish with unsalted butter and keep it warm close to the stove.

When the water is boiling, drop in the gnocchi and boil them until they float to the top, 3 or 4 minutes. Retrieve them with the slotted spoon and place them on the perforated tray. You are, in essence, trying to "drip-dry" them. After several minutes, transfer the gnocchi to the serving dish. You will find that it is quicker to make, cook, and drain the gnocchi all at once, rather than to do one stage for all the dough sections at a time. Do not layer the gnocchi; try to keep them separated in the serving dish to prevent them from clinging together.

When all the gnocchi are cooked, put them in a 200 degree F oven, loosely covered, until the sauce is ready. They will keep in the oven for about 30 minutes. Serve topped with the *pastissada*.

Note: Gnocchi can be made in advance, arranged on trays, put into the freezer until they are solid, and transferred in their frozen state to a freezer bag. Freeze for up to 6 months.

Bigoli with Smoked Sausage
and Borlotti Beans

bigoli alla contadina

FOR 4 PEOPLE

5 tablespoons extra-virgin olive oil

4 large cloves garlic, minced

8 ounces *lugana* or *luganega* sausage,
thinly sliced

3 cups drained, cooked or canned *borlotti*
beans or Lamon beans

1/2 cup bean-cooking liquid or canned bean
liquid thinned with water

1 cup homemade meat broth or good-quality
chicken broth

1 pound fresh *bigoli* or imported Italian
dried *bucatini*, penne, or *perciatelli*

2 tablespoons kosher salt

3 tablespoons chopped fresh Italian parsley

freshly ground black pepper

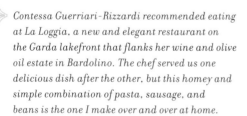

*Contessa Guerriari-Rizzardi recommended eating
at La Loggia, a new and elegant restaurant on
the Garda lakefront that flanks her wine and olive
oil estate in Bardolino. The chef served us one
delicious dish after the other, but this homey and
simple combination of pasta, sausage, and
beans is the one I make over and over at home.*

If lugana *sausage is not available, substitute*
luganega *or another high-quality mild smoked
sausage.* Lugana *is a thin sausage, so if you
are replacing it with a thicker one, it should be
cut in half lengthwise before slicing, or it will
collect at the bottom of the pasta dish instead of
finding its way into the sauce with the other
ingredients.*

In a wide skillet large enough to accommodate the cooked
pasta later, warm the olive oil over medium-low heat.
Add the garlic and sausage and sauté. When the garlic is
well softened and fragrant and the sausage is lightly
browned, after about 7 minutes, add the beans. Using a
wooden spoon, stir them with the oil and break them up a
little. Stir in the bean liquid and the meat broth. Simmer,
uncovered, over medium-low heat until the liquid has
thickened to a sauce consistency, about 20 minutes.

Meanwhile, bring a large pot filled with water to a rolling
boil. Stir in the pasta and the kosher salt. Cook, always
over the highest possible heat and stirring constantly to
prevent the strands from sticking together, until the pasta
is almost cooked. Cooking time depends on what type
of pasta is used. Fresh *bigoli* are cooked as soon as the
water returns to the boil and the noodles rise to the surface,
about 3 minutes. Factory-made *bucatini* cook quickly
because they are hollow and their walls are thin, no more
than 7 minutes. Penne or *perciatelli* usually take another
minute or two to cook.

Add a glass of cold water to the pot to arrest the boiling
and drain immediately. Transfer the pasta to the skillet
with the bean sauce. Toss together over high heat with the
parsley and plenty of pepper. Serve immediately.

Spaghettini with Little Shrimp
in the Style of Venice

spaghettini cóe conòce

FOR 3 PEOPLE

1 pound shrimp (see recipe introduction)

5 tablespoons extra-virgin olive oil

3 large cloves garlic, minced

3-inch-long strip lemon zest

2 cups packed fresh or canned peeled plum tomatoes, halved and seeded

pinch of red pepper flakes

2 tablespoons chopped fresh Italian parsley

$1/_4$ teaspoon sea salt

12 ounces imported Italian spaghettini, thin linguine, or spaghetti

2 tablespoons kosher salt

 Here is a popular Venetian pasta dish made with tiny little shrimp called conòce *in the local dialect. If fresh tiny shrimp cannot be found, use small or medium-size shrimp and chop them up after cleaning them. The shells from the shrimp are boiled in the water that will later be used for cooking the pasta, which adds some flavor of the sea.*

Rinse the shrimp in cold running water and drain well. Peel the shrimp, setting the shells aside. Using a paring knife, make a slit along the top side of each shrimp and remove the dark intestinal vein; rinse under cool running water to clean thoroughly. If using tiny shrimp, keep them whole; if using small or medium shrimp, cut them into small pieces. Put the shells in an ample pot with 5 quarts of water and bring to a boil; reduce the heat to a steady simmer.

In an ample skillet, warm 3 tablespoons of the olive oil, the garlic, and the lemon zest over low heat until the garlic is nicely softened but not colored, about 2 minutes. Add the tomatoes and red pepper flakes and simmer for 20 minutes. Remove and discard the lemon zest and add the shrimp. Continue to simmer until the shrimp are cooked through but not overcooked, about 1 minute. Remove the skillet from the heat and add the parsley and sea salt. Taste and adjust the seasonings. Cover to keep warm.

Use a slotted spoon or wire skimmer to remove the shells from the pot in which they have been simmering. Bring the water to a rolling boil and stir in the pasta and kosher salt. Cook, always over the highest heat possible and stirring constantly to prevent the pasta strands from sticking together, until the pasta is almost cooked, about 5 minutes.

Add a glass of cold water to the pot to arrest the boiling and drain immediately. Transfer the pasta to the skillet with the sauce, add the remaining 2 tablespoons olive oil, and return the skillet to high heat. Use 2 long forks to distribute all the ingredients evenly, about 1 minute. Serve immediately.

Spaghetti with Radicchio

spaghetti al radicchio

FOR 2 TO 4 PEOPLE

6 tablespoons extra-virgin olive oil

1 red onion, thinly sliced and chopped

1 head radicchio (8 to 10 ounces),
cut into julienne and then roughly chopped

$1/2$ cup hot water

$1/2$ teaspoon sea salt

12 ounces imported Italian spaghetti

$1^1/2$ tablespoons kosher salt

freshly ground coarse black pepper

I corresponded with Paolo Lanapoppi, a Venetian writer, gondola restorer, and circumscribed sailor, for some time before I finally tracked him down in Venice. He had suggested a chat over a cappuccino, but when I arrived in nearby Verona, he, like most other native Venetians, had evacuated the city until the carnival delirium was over. When I returned some months later, he was busy writing, and restoring an old ketch berthed in Chioggia, preparing it for the summer regatta in the lagoon. Knowing that I was writing a cookbook, he had protested that he wasn't a cook at all, so not to expect any gastronomic material from him. But the radicchio of nearby Treviso was in full flower, and he cooked up this delightful dish for lunch over talk of carnevale, sailboats, *and books. I have been making it ever since whenever I can find radicchio for an affordable price in my local markets.*

In an ample skillet, warm the olive oil over medium-low heat. Add the onion and sauté until nicely softened and lightly colored, about 6 minutes. Toss in the radicchio and use a wooden spoon to coat it evenly in the olive oil. Add the water, continuing to toss. Cover and continue to cook over medium-low heat, stirring occasionally, until the radicchio is tender, 10 to 12 minutes. Add the sea salt, cover, and set aside.

Bring a large pot filled with water over high heat to a rolling boil. Stir in the pasta and kosher salt. Cook, always over the highest heat possible and stirring constantly to prevent the pasta strands from sticking together, until the spaghetti is almost cooked, about 6 minutes.

Add a glass of cold water to the pot to arrest the boiling and drain immediately, setting aside about 1 cup of the cooking water. Add the spaghetti to the skillet with the cooked radicchio and return the skillet to high heat. Use 2 long forks to distribute all the ingredients evenly, about 1 minute. If necessary, add a little of the pasta-cooking water to moisten so that everything mixes nicely together. Serve immediately with plenty of pepper.

Note: Paolo topped the pasta generously with Parmigiano-Reggiano cheese at the table, but I think the pleasantly bitter flavor of the radicchio comes through more clearly without it.

Beet-Stuffed Pasta with Poppy Seeds and Smoked Ricotta

cazunzièi alle rape rosse con ricotta affumicata

FOR 6 PEOPLE

FOR THE FILLING:

1 pound red beets

1 $1/4$ pounds baking potatoes

$1/2$ teaspoon ground cinnamon

$1/2$ teaspoon sea salt

freshly ground white pepper

$1/4$ cup unsalted butter

1 large onion, garted or finely chopped

2 tablespoons bread crumbs

1 egg yolk

$1/3$ cup grated *grana,* or Parmigiano-Reggiano cheese

FOR THE PASTA:

I pound homemade egg pasta dough (recipe of your choice)

1 egg white

cornmeal or all-purpose flour for sprinkling

2 tablespoons coarse salt

8 tablespoons unsalted butter, melted

$1/4$ pound smoked ricotta, shaved or crumbled (see recipe head note)

$1/4$ cup poppy seeds for sprinkling over pasta

Cazunzièi, are a specialty of the mountainous Cadore and Ampezzo regions of Belluno Province. The beet-and-potato stuffed pasta pillows are always finished off with melted sweet butter and a scattering of poppy seeds, an Austrian touch. As in this recipe, they may be further embellished with shaved smoked ricotta, a unique local pressed cheese with the texture of feta cheese. (Lacking smoked ricotta, which is difficult to procure outside of Italy, I have substituted ricotta salata, baked smoked ricotta, or baked unsmoked ricotta cheese—or even the French aged goat's cheese, Boucheron— with a different but pleasant result).

To make the filling, preheat the oven to 450 degrees F. Cut the green tops off the beets, leaving about 1/2 inch of the stem intact. Scrub the beets, but do not peel, and place them with the potatoes on a baking sheet. Roast until the beets and the potatoes are thoroughly tender, 30 to 40 minutes, or until a knife can pierce them easily. The cooking time will depend on the size; large ones may need up to 15 minutes more to cook. Permit the beets and potatoes to cool until they can be handled, then peel them. Pass the potatoes through a potato ricer or finely mash with a fork. Finely chop the beets by hand or in a food processor. In a medium bowl, combine the potatoes, beets, cinnamon, salt, and pepper to taste. In an ample skillet over low heat, warm the butter. Add the onion and sauté until well softened, 3 to 4 minutes. Stir in the bread crumbs. Add the potato-beet mixture and sauté, tossing to combine well and to evaporate excess moisture from the beets, about 4 minutes. Transfer the mixture to the bowl. When it has cooled, mix in the yolk and grated cheese. To give the filling a uniform consistency, pass the mixture through a food mill, or beat it well in the bowl of an electric mixer. Set it aside.

continued

Beet-Stuffed Pasta with Poppy Seeds and Smoked Ricotta

continued

To make the cazunzièi, divide the pasta dough into four equal pieces. Work with only one strip of dough at a time. Keep the remaining portions of dough covered with an inverted bowl until you are ready to use them to prevent it from becoming dry. Roll a section of dough out, finally passing it through the last setting of the pasta machine for the thinnest possible dough. Tears in the dough can be easily remedied by folding the dough into thirds and passing it through the rollers again.

Cut one strip of dough in half crosswise; keep the other half covered with a damp cloth. Put the egg white in a small bowl. Working quickly, place a teaspoonful of filling at 2-inch intervals in rows along one half of the pasta strip.

To ensure a strong seal, dip a pastry brush in the egg white and paint a grid between and around the mounds of filling, so that each one is surrounded by a square of egg white. Place the second half of the pasta strip over the filled sheet. Press down firmly around each mound of filling to seal the bundles, forcing out any trapped pockets of air.

Use a fluted pastry wheel or a knife to cut 2-inch square cazunzièi along the egg white lines. Press down around each bundle to secure the seal. Repeat with the remaining dough and filling.

Place the cazunzièi on a tray covered with a clean kitchen towel sprinkled with a little cornmeal or flour. Keep them from overlapping to prevent them from sticking together. Turn them occasionally so they dry evenly and don't stick to the tray. They should not be left to dry longer than 30 minutes before being cooked, refrigerated, or frozen.

If freezing the cazunzièi, do so immediately in the following way: Place them on parchment or foil-lined trays that will fit into your freezer space; arrange the trays so that the disks cannot touch each other during freezing. When they are thoroughly frozen, they should be removed from the trays, slipped into freezer bags, and returned to the freezer until ready to use, up to about 3 months.

Have ready 2 warmed, wide, shallow serving platters. Bring a large pot filled with water to a rapid boil. Add the coarse salt. Pick up the cloths on which the cazunzièi are resting, grabbing two corners in each hand, and tip them all directly into the rapidly boiling water; stir. Keep the heat at high and cover the pot until the water returns to a boil.

Cook gently to prevent them from breaking, about 2 to 4 minutes once the water has returned to a boil, stirring carefully. Using a wire skimmer or slotted spoon, lift the cazunzièi out as they rise to surface, shaking off the excess water. Transfer to a serving platter, spreading them out rather than piling them to prevent them from breaking.

When all the cazunzièi are cooked, anoint them with the melted butter and scatter the shaved cheese over the top. Finally, sprinkle lightly with the poppy seeds. Serve immediately.

Tagliolini with Shrimp
and Broccoli Rabe from Burano

tagliolini coi gamberetti e cime di rapa

FOR 4 TO 5 PEOPLE

1 pound small shrimp

1 bunch broccoli rabe (about 1¹/₄ pounds)

6 tablespoons extra-virgin olive oil

4 large cloves garlic, minced

3 tablespoons kosher salt

1 pound homemade egg pasta
or imported Italian dried tagliatelle (marked
pasta all'uovo, dried linguine, or *nidi*)

sea salt

freshly ground white or black pepper

*While strolling through the central thoroughfare
of Burano, a smiling woman standing in the
doorway of the Trattoria Da Primo beckoned me to
enter. I was compelled to take a detour from my
destination, the legendary Da Romano restaurant
on the island. She seated me at a table and took
things in hand. "We bought shrimp from the
fishermen this morning," she offered, "and the
broccoletti di rape was picked today. I can cook
them for you with tagliolini," she added. The
combination would not have occurred to me without some thought, but it was a lovely composition
of flavors. (Note: The tagliolini were actually
tagliatelle—I found this curious use of the term
tagliolini interchanged with tagliatelle commonplace in the Veneto.)*

Rinse the shrimp in cold running water and drain well.
Peel the shrimp and discard the shells. Using a paring
knife, make a slit along the top side of each shrimp
and remove the dark intestinal vein; rinse under warm
running water to clean thoroughly. Set the shrimp aside.

Immerse the greens in water and swish them well to
remove any sand. Cut the tough tips off the stems and peel
the stems, just as you would asparagus. Use a large knife
to chop the greens crosswise into 3 parts, thus shortening
them to make them manageable for eating.

In an ample skillet, combine the olive oil and garlic and
warm over low heat until the garlic is well softened
and cooked through but only barely colored, about 2 minutes. Raise the heat to high and immediately stir in the
shrimp. Use a wooden spoon to separate the shrimp
so that they have plenty of room to cook evenly. When they
just turn pink, toss them to cook them on the reverse
side. When they have cooked through and there is plenty
of liquid from the shrimp in the pan, after about 3 minutes
total, remove the skillet from the heat and set it aside.

Bring a large pot filled with water to a rolling boil. Add
the kosher salt and greens and stir immediately. If using
dried pasta, also add it now. If using fresh pasta, do
not add it until the greens have cooked for about 4 minutes,
then slip it in, stirring. Cook, always over the highest
heat possible and stirring constantly to prevent the strands
from sticking together, until almost cooked. Fresh
tagliolini are ready when they float to the surface, about
2 minutes after the water returns to a boil. For dried
tagliatelle, read package instructions carefully and cook
about 1 minute less than the cooking time indicated.

continued

Tagliolini with Shrimp
and Broccoli Rabe from Burano
continued

Add a glass of cold water to the pot to arrest the boiling and drain immediately, setting aside about 1 cup of the cooking water. Do not overdrain, that is, allow some of the cooking water to still be dripping from the greens and the pasta.

Add the pasta and greens to the skillet with the shrimp and return the skillet to high heat. Use 2 long forks to distribute all the ingredients evenly, about 1 minute. If necessary, add a little of the pasta-cooking water to moisten so that everything mixes nicely together. Season with sea salt and pepper and serve immediately.

Tagliatelle with Radicchio,
Onion, and Clams

*tagliatelle al radicchio
con cipolla e vongole*

FOR 4 TO 6 PEOPLE

2 pounds cockles, or 2 dozen very small littleneck clams

4 tablespoons ($^1/_2$ stick) unsalted butter

3 tablespoons extra-virgin olive oil

1 large onion, thinly sliced and chopped

1 head radicchio (8 to 10 ounces), cut into julienne and then roughly chopped

$^1/_2$ teaspoon sea salt

1 pound homemade egg pasta or imported Italian dried tagliatelle (marked *pasta all'uovo, dried linguine,* or *nidi*)

2 tablespoons kosher salt

freshly ground coarse black pepper

It was the season for radicchio when Mauro Stoppa, skipper and chef of the sailboat the Eolo, *brought me to Chioggia, the real fish capital of the Venetian lagoon. His favorite local place was the Osteria Penzo, a stone's throw from the water's edge. The proprietor, Giuseppe Ardizzon, puts together radicchio and clams with tagliatelle—for me, a new and startling combination of flavors. It was a delightful pairing of land and sea, made all the more delicious because the tagliatelle had been freshly made.*

With a very stiff brush, scrub the shellfish. Rinse well and place in a large bowl with cold water to cover. Let soak for up to 1 hour to cleanse them of any sand. Drain and rinse, discarding any shellfish that do not close to the touch.

In a very large skillet, melt the butter with the olive oil over medium-low heat. Add the onion and sauté until well softened but not browned, about 5 minutes. Add the radicchio and toss well to coat; immediately add the cleaned shellfish and cover tightly. Cook over medium heat until the radicchio is tender and the shellfish open fully, about 10 minutes. Remove from the heat immediately, then remove the lid to prevent further cooking. Discard any unopened shellfish. Add the sea salt and toss to mix.

While the sauce is cooking, bring a large pot filled with water to a rolling boil. Stir in the pasta and kosher salt. Cook, always over the highest heat possible and stirring constantly to prevent the strands from sticking together, until almost cooked. Fresh tagliolini are ready when they float to the surface, about 2 minutes after the water returns to a boil. For dried pasta, read package instructions and cook about 1 minute less than the cooking time indicated.

Add a glass of cold water to the pot to arrest the boiling and drain immediately. Add the pasta to the skillet with the radicchio and shellfish and return it to high heat. Use 2 long forks to distribute all the ingredients evenly, about 1 minute. Serve at once with a little pepper. Grated cheese is unthinkable here.

Rice and Peas in the Style
of Corte Sconta

risi e bisi

FOR 4 TO 6 PEOPLE

1 pound organic peas, shelled (1 1/4 cups shelled peas), pods reserved for stock, or 8 ounces frozen premium petite peas

4 cups meat broth or good-quality chicken broth, or 6 cups if not using stock from pea pods (see recipe introduction)

5 tablespoons unsalted butter

1 tablespoon extra-virgin olive oil

1 onion, chopped

2 ounces pancetta, chopped

3 tablespoons chopped fresh Italian parsley (optional)

1 1/2 cups *vialone nano, carnaroli,* or *arborio* rice

1/2 cup dry white wine

sea salt

freshly grated Parmigiano-Reggiano cheese (optional)

 Risi e bisi is ubiquitous in Venice in springtime, when the new peas of the season appear in the markets. It is without a doubt the most famous of all Venetian dishes. Fresh peas are at their sugary prime for only a few days at the most, thus the authentic risi e bisi *is not an easy dish to make in the American kitchen. Nevertheless, I cannot resist offering this recipe, which was kindly given to me by Rita Pro, who, with her husband, Claudio, runs Corte Sconta, a trattoria in Venice.*

Like all Venetian risottos, this dish should be all'onda, *quite soupy, but not actually a soup. In Venice, Rita buys local peas grown without pesticides or other chemicals, shells them, and boils the pods to make a tasty stock for cooking the rice. This is advisable only if you are certain the peas you procure are organic or if you grow your own. If not using pod stock, increase the meat broth to about 6 cups.*

In the absence of freshly picked peas, a good facsimile of risi e bisi *can be made with frozen petite peas. Rita's version does not include parsley, but many traditional Venetian recipes do.*

If making the pea-pod stock, place the pods in a pot with cold water to cover by 3 inches. Bring to a boil over high heat, cover, reduce the heat to medium-low, and simmer until the liquid is reduced to about 2 cups and the pods are very mushy, about 4 hours. Pass the liquid and pods through a food mill, then combine with the meat broth in a large saucepan. Place the pan on a back burner of the stove and heat just until hot.

In a large, wide skillet, warm 3 tablespoons of the butter with the olive oil over medium-low heat. Add the onion and pancetta and sauté gently until the pancetta is nicely colored and the onion is thoroughly softened and fragrant, about 4 minutes. Stir in 1 tablespoon of the parsley, if using. Stir in the rice with a wooden spoon, mixing it well with the other ingredients in the pan. Cook over medium heat for about 4 minutes, stirring occasionally to coat the rice well. As soon as the grains "click" as they are stirred, stir in the wine. When it has been fully absorbed and the alcohol has evaporated, after about 3 minutes, add a ladleful of the broth, followed by the peas (adding the peas with the broth at this point prevents their skins from toughening). When the broth is absorbed, add another ladleful of the hot broth to the rice and cook and stir, until it, too, is absorbed. Stir occasionally to blend the broth with the other ingredients, but not constantly, as continuous stirring only releases more starch into the risotto. Continue to add the hot broth, a ladleful at a time, until the rice is tender, 20 to 25 minutes. At the end, the mixture should be very moist, with a somewhat soupy consistency.

Remove the skillet from the heat and taste the risotto for salt. Stir in the remaining 2 tablespoons butter and fold in the remaining 2 tablespoons parsley, if using. Serve immediately. Grated Parmigiano, if using, should be added at the table.

GOLDEN RULES FOR MAKING A PROPER RISOTTO

1. *Use the correct type of rice for the dish being prepared.*

2. *Use a pan with adequate surface area. An ample copper skillet is ideal because it retains heat well and distributes it evenly throughout cooking. Second best is a wide, thick-bottomed, good-quality skillet.*

3. *Use a wooden spoon to stir occasionally, working from the center of the pan outward, always in the same direction. Mix it as little as possible. The rice should be folded rather than turned to avoid stirring up too much starch.*

4. *A risotto is only as good as the broth and the other ingredients from which it is made. It is preferable to prepare broth from scratch using fresh ingredients.*

5. *Thoroughly saute any* battuto, *that is, a chopped vegetable base of carrot, onion, and celery, to soften it completely.*

6. *Never use substitutes for genuine cheese to finish off a risotto. Parmigiano-Reggiano should never be cooked in the risotto. Rather, fold it in carefully once the risotto is taken off the stove top.*

7. *A proper risotto is made al minuto, "to the minute," that is, just before it is eaten. True risotto cannot be cooked ahead of time.*

Rice Cooked in Milk

riso con latte

FOR 2 PEOPLE

FOR THE SAVORY VERSION:

4 cups milk

1 cup *vialone nano* rice

$^1/_2$ teaspoon sea salt

unsalted butter

freshly grated Parmigiano-Reggiano cheese
(optional)

FOR THE SWEET VERSION:

$3^1/_2$ cups milk

1 cup *vialone nano* rice

$^1/_2$ teaspoon sea salt

sugar

 Perhaps the best way to experience the wonderful vialone nano rice of the Veneto is in the simplest preparation. Vialone nano cooked in milk is the first recipe Venice-born Nicoletta Polo suggested to me when we talked about Venetian food. She added the caveat that the dish required the true rice of the Veneto, as only vialone nano will soften through and through, creating the correct texture.

This dish is Venetian comfort food. In my mind, it falls into the same category as the steaming bowl of pastina, milk, and butter that Italian children grow up on and the proverbial chicken soup—nourishing, healthful, digestible, and delicious—of countless cultures. Venetian children love riso con latte, with sugar for breakfast, for an afterschool snack, or even for dinner. Be sure to add the salt only after cooking to avoid inadvertently oversalting.

If you are making the savory version, the quantities called for should stand. If you are making the sweet version, however, it should not be as soupy, but instead more like a risotto. To achieve this, decrease the milk by about ½ cup or increase the rice by ¼ cup. If you are making a plain version, neither savory nor sweet, the quantities should also stand.

In a saucepan, bring the milk to a gentle boil over medium-low heat. Stir in the rice. Simmer, stirring occasionally, until the rice is soft, about 10 minutes. Stir in the salt. Season to taste with butter and cheese for the savory version, or with sugar for the sweet version, or eat without seasoning.

Rice in Cavroman

riso in cavroman

FOR 4 PEOPLE

3 tablespoons unsalted butter

2 tablespoons extra-virgin olive oil

1 large onion, finely chopped

1 celery stalk, including leaves,
finely chopped

1 large carrot, peeled and finely chopped

1 pound boneless stewing mutton or lamb,
trimmed of any fat and gristle and diced

2 fresh or canned plum tomatoes,
peeled, seeded, and chopped
or $1/3$ cup tomato sauce

3 fresh sage leaves or $1/2$ teaspoon
crumbled dried sage

1 cinnamon stick or $1/4$ teaspoon ground
cinnamon

$1/8$ teaspoon freshly grated nutmeg

2 whole cloves

1 teaspoon sea salt

freshly ground black pepper

about $2^1/2$ cups hot water, homemade
meat broth, or good-quality purchased
chicken broth

1 cup *vialone nano* rice

 With its cinnamon, nutmeg, and cloves, this substantial Venetian dish evokes the flavors of the Levant. It is also made without the rice, served as a meat course. Then it is called il cavroman and is accompanied by potatoes and onions. As for what cavroman means, even the Venetians are befuddled. In his tome on the Venetian kitchen, A tola co i nostri veci: la cucina veneziana, Mariù Salvatori de Zuliani conjectures that it came from cavra, or cavrer, or even cavaron, or finally, caprone castrato, "castrated goat" in the country dialect. Whatever its derivation, riso in cavroman has come to mean a beguiling risotto of mutton or lamb that has been popular in Venice and its provinces since before the days of the doges.

In an ample skillet, warm the butter with the olive oil over medium-low heat. Add the onion, celery, and carrot and sauté until softened, about 10 minutes. Raise the heat to medium, add the meat, and sauté until it is nicely colored, about 10 minutes. Stir in the tomatoes, sage, cinnamon, nutmeg, cloves, salt, pepper to taste, and 1 cup of the water. Cover, reduce the heat to medium-low, and simmer, stirring occasionally and always replacing the lid, until the meat is tender, 30 to 45 minutes. Fish out and discard the cinnamon stick.

Stir in the rice and the remaining $1^1/2$ cups water, cover, and cook until the rice is tender, about 15 minutes. The rice grains should be tender but still firm at the center. Serve hot.

Risotto with Pumpkin and Walnuts

risotto di zucca gialla con le noci

FOR 4 PEOPLE

about 5 cups homemade meat broth
or good-quality purchased chicken broth

4 tablespoons ($^1/_2$ stick) unsalted butter

4 tablespoons extra-virgin olive oil

4 cups peeled, finely diced sugar pumpkin,
calabaza, or butternut squash

1 large onion, finely chopped

2 cups *vialone nano, carnaroli,*
or *arborio* rice

$^1/_2$ cup Amarone wine

sea salt

freshly ground white or black pepper

$^3/_4$ cup walnuts, chopped

freshly grated Parmigiano-Reggiano cheese

 *Fabrizio DeVenosa, chef of La Loggia in Bardolino,
has contributed this recipe. The Amarone tem-
pers slightly the sweetness of the pumpkin. After
using a small amount in the risotto, the rest
of the Amarone should be drunk at the table. It
is best to use tasty, homemade meat broth because,
as the Italian saying goes, "good with good
makes good." But if necessary, substitute good-
quality purchased chicken broth.*

Place the meat broth in a saucepan on a burner behind
or next to the one on which you will cook the risotto,
keeping it hot for the entire cooking time. In a large, wide
skillet, warm half of the butter with half of the oil over
medium-low heat. Add the squash and sauté until it
is nicely colored all over, about 10 minutes. Cover the pan
and cook over medium-low heat until thoroughly softened, about 30 minutes. Remove from the heat and use
a fork or a potato masher to mash the cooked squash thoroughly. Keep hot.

Meanwhile, in another ample skillet, warm the remaining
butter and oil over medium to medium-low heat. Add
the onion and sauté until it is nicely colored and completely softened, about 5 minutes. With a wooden spoon,
stir in the rice to coat and heat it evenly, about 3 minutes.
Stir in the wine. When it has been fully absorbed and
the alcohol has evaporated, after about 3 minutes, add a
ladleful of the hot broth to the rice and cook and stir until
it, too, is absorbed. When half the broth has been used
up (and the rice is half cooked), stir in the squash, which
must still be hot. Add another ladleful of broth, following
the same procedure of ensuring that it is absorbed by
the rice before adding more. Continue to add the hot
broth, a ladleful at a time, until the rice is tender, which
should take about 25 minutes total. At the end, the
risotto should be very moist, almost wet, and the rice
grains should be tender but still firm at the center.

Remove the skillet from the heat and taste for salt. Using
a spatula, fold in the pepper to taste and half of the walnuts.
Transfer the risotto to a warmed wide, shallow serving
bowl, strew the remaining walnuts over the top, and
sprinkle with cheese. Serve immediately, passing additional cheese at the table.

Risotto with Red Radicchio of Verona

risotto al radicchio rosso di Verona

FOR 5 OR 6 PEOPLE

about 5 cups homemade meat broth
or good-quality purchased chicken broth

8 ounces red radicchio

3 tablespoons unsalted butter

3 tablespoons extra-virgin olive oil

1 large red onion, finely chopped

1 clove garlic, minced

2 cups *vialone nano* rice

$1/2$ cup Soave or other dry white wine

sea salt

freshly ground white or black pepper

freshly grated Parmigiano-Reggiano cheese

walnut halves for garnish (optional)

A lovely pink risotto results from the combination of the rice and the radicchio. The flavor is particular—delicate with an ever so slight, pleasant bitterness.

Place the broth in a saucepan on a back burner, keeping it hot for the entire cooking time. Slice the radicchio in half lengthwise and cut out the tough core from each one. Slice crosswise into fine julienne, then chop roughly. In a large, wide skillet, warm half of the butter with half of the olive oil over low heat. Add the onion and garlic and sauté until completely softened, about 4 minutes. Raise the heat to medium and add the radicchio. Sauté, tossing to cook it evenly, for 5 minutes. Remove about 5 tablespoons of the radicchio and set aside. Cover the pan partially and continue to cook, tossing the radicchio frequently and always replacing the lid, until tender, about 10 minutes. Remove the radicchio mixture from the pan.

In the same skillet, warm the remaining butter and oil over medium heat until hot but not browned, about 1 minute. With a wooden spoon, stir in the rice to coat it and heat it evenly, about 3 minutes. Return the radicchio mixture to the skillet and toss with the rice. Stir in the wine. When it has been fully absorbed, add a ladleful of the broth and stir again. When the broth is absorbed, stir in another ladleful of the broth and cook until it, too, is absorbed. Continue to add the hot broth, a ladleful at a time, until the rice is tender, about 25 minutes total. At the end, the risotto should be very loose, and the rice grains tender but still firm at the center.

Remove the skillet from the heat and taste for salt. Stir in pepper to taste. Transfer the risotto to a warmed wide, shallow serving bowl, strew the radicchio that has been set aside over the top, and sprinkle lightly with grated cheese. Garnish with walnuts, if using. Serve immediately, passing additional cheese at the table.

4

Polenta

*Building painted with a food-
store sign in Cortina d'Ampezzo*

One day, not far from the Ca' d'Oro *traghetto* stop, I noticed a small glassmaker's shop that stood out from all the rest. Unlike most others all over Venice, which are polished, elegant, dazzling, this one had a simple window display of a few very old and interesting vases. An elderly man stood at the doorway, and I entered. As we chatted, it became obvious to me that, in a sense, he was his window display. He lamented how things had changed, in Venice, in Italy; how much more beautiful the glassmaking was once, how much more precious the glassmaker's art. "Everything has gone to the communists," he said. "People care only about money. They just don't like to make it," he expanded. "They like other people to make it for them." His thoughts soon turned to food—the usual turn of events anywhere in Italy. "Now even the poor people eat everything," he continued. "When I was growing up, we had that blessed slab of polenta *abbrustolita* [charred over the fire], and it was God's food. It was so good. Now we all eat *bistecca*, and I prefer the slab of polenta. It hasn't changed, it's still God's food."

My conversation with the old man reminded me of an amusing story I had once read when researching the history of meat consumption in northern Italy. At the end of the nineteenth century, a benevolent nobleman decided to give his peasants some meat from his pantry. He apportioned out a generous amount to each one of them. Soon after, however, he discovered that they sold their meat to buy polenta instead.

Not surprisingly, the origin of the Veneto's beloved polenta has a long history that reaches back to the ancient *puls*, or porridge, of the Romans. Long before corn was brought from the New World, barley meal, ground dried fava beans, or buckwheat was cooked into porridge. During the Middle Ages, polenta took the form of pounded favas boiled with oil, onion, and sage, or figs and honey. Corn polenta, however, became the primary staple of the Veneto once the grain was introduced. The poor ate it plain, perhaps with cheese, when there was any. But polenta had no class distinctions. Wealthy households ate it, too, adding condiments to it or making it into more elaborate dishes.

Polenta warrants a discussion on its own not only because of its importance in the diet of the Veneto, but also because it doesn't fit any particular course category. It may appear in toast form as an appetizer, in slabs as the mainstay of a meal, or loose, like porridge, alongside a dish that will flavor its edges with its gravy or sauce. At one time, polenta was eaten for every meal and accompanied virtually every dish. Today, bread, a ready food, has replaced polenta to a large extent. But there are still certain dishes with which only polenta is eaten. Among them are preparations made with *seppie* (cuttlefish) or sautéed wild mushrooms (with melted fresh cheese called *skiz* alongside), as well as other dishes in this chapter.

Notes on Cooking Polenta

Traditionally, a special copper pot called a *paiolo* and a heavy wooden spoon are used for making polenta, but any good-quality, heavy-bottomed pot will do. Because so much stirring is involved, it is helpful to use a wooden spoon with a long handle to avoid splattering and burning a hand held too close to the surface of the polenta. The whisk is not commonly used in Italy, and it is even considered heretical to the Italian kitchen by purists, but I find that a strong whisk turns out a fine, lump-free polenta. The secret is not as much in the instrument as it is in the method: devoted, nonstop, energetic stirring is essential for perfect results. Always stir in the same direction to keep the texture smooth and uniform. If the polenta seems to be drying out before it is cooked, add boiling water to it, a little at a time, to keep it soft and to be able to keep stirring. It is ready when it pulls away from the sides of the pan easily.

Basic Polenta

polenta

FOR 6 PEOPLE

7 cups cold water

1 tablespoon kosher salt

2 cups coarse polenta

boiling water, if needed

If you cannot find imported Italian cornmeal for polenta, Spanish ground cornmeal marketed by Goya and other Latin food companies is a fine substitute. These cornmeals come in fine or coarse grind, and a good texture for polenta can be made from a combination of the two in equal parts. An imported Italian instant polenta that cooks in five minutes is available, but it is expensive and thickens and cooks so quickly that lumps form before the polenta can be stirred properly. (Important: Do not confuse ordinary cornmeal for muffins and the like with polenta cornmeal.)

In traditional preparation, you add polenta to boiling water in a slow, steady trickle, stirring all the while to prevent lumps from forming. A richer polenta, cooked in milk instead of water, is made the same way, but it is usually sprinkled with sugar and cinnamon for a snack or sweet dish.

In a large saucepan, bring the water to a rapid boil over high heat. Add the kosher salt, then slowly pour in the polenta while stirring constantly with a long-handled wooden spoon or a whisk. Reduce the heat to medium-low and, using the wooden spoon or whisk, stir constantly in the same direction to prevent lumps from forming and to keep the boiling temperature constant. This is important if the polenta is to become properly soft and creamy. The polenta is cooked when it is so thick that it begins to resist stirring and pulls away from the sides of the pan with the spoon or whisk, usually after about 30 minutes. If the polenta is quite thick but still not pulling away easily from the pan, add a little more boiling water and continue to stir until it is ready. Pour into a warmed serving dish or directly on the plates if serving alongside shrimp (page 98) or salt cod (page 94).

Grilled or Fried Polenta

As soon as the polenta is cooked, pour it onto an oiled marble slab, cutting board, or other flat work surface, and use a rubber spatula to spread it evenly about ¼ inch thick. Dip the spatula into a glass of cold water as you work to prevent the polenta from sticking to it. Permit the polenta to set fully, about 30 minutes. Use a knife or cake spatula to cut it into squares about the size of bread slices or into the size or shape desired. Brush the pieces lightly on both sides with olive oil. Run them under a broiler until they are lightly charred or blistered on both sides or fry them on both sides in olive oil or butter.

Polenta can also be poured into a greased mold to set. To cut, turn it out onto a work surface and slice it with nylon thread, fishing line, or unflavored dental floss. The slices can be grilled or fried in olive oil or butter.

Polenta with Salt Cod
in the Manner of Vicenza

polenta con baccalà alla vicentina

FOR 5 TO 6 PEOPLE

2 pounds meaty white salt cod fillets

$1/2$ cup unbleached flour

2 tablespoons unsalted butter

1 onion, finely chopped

2 cloves garlic, minced

5 anchovy fillets packed in olive oil, finely chopped

1 tablespoon minced fresh Italian parsley

$1/3$ cup extra-virgin olive oil

$1/3$ cup freshly grated Parmigiano-Reggiano cheese

1 cup dry white wine

1 cup milk, warmed until tepid

Basic Polenta (page 92)

An old Hebrew recipe, this dish is probably the most famous way to cook baccalà *in the Veneto. It was not adopted by the majority of the population because the Catholic Church, in order to curb excess, prohibited the use of cheese and milk in the same dish. Vicenza adopted the recipe in the beginning of the twentieth century, and it has since experienced a meteoric rise in popularity throughout the region.*

Two days before serving this dish, immerse the salt cod in an ample bowl in cold water to cover. Cover and refrigerate for about 48 hours, depending on the thickness of the fillets, and change the water once or twice each day.

Drain the rehydrated fillets and rinse under cold running water. Remove any errant skin and bones, then immerse the fillets, one at a time, into boiling water for 2 minutes. This extra step ensures that the cod will be firm, yet tender once it is cooked. Allow the fillets to cool completely, then cut them crosswise into 3-inch pieces, patting each piece dry with paper towels. The fish should be as dry as possible so as not to absorb excess flour.

Spread the flour on a sheet of waxed paper or a large plate and have the fish pieces alongside.

In a small skillet, warm the butter over medium-low heat. Add the onion, garlic, anchovies, and parsley and sauté until the onion and garlic are well softened but not browned, about 5 minutes. Remove from the heat.

In a heavy-bottomed, ample skillet large enough to accommodate all the fish pieces with ease, warm the olive oil over medium heat until it is sizzling hot. Meanwhile, lightly dredge the pieces of salt cod in the flour, dusting off excess flour from each piece before placing it in the hot oil. It is essential that the skillet is large enough to accommodate all of the fish pieces without crowding to ensure that each is browned evenly and thoroughly. After the pieces are nicely browned on all sides, about 10 minutes, sprinkle them evenly with the cheese and the onion mixture without disturbing the salt cod. Add the wine, reduce the heat to medium-low, and permit the alcohol to evaporate, about 3 minutes. Now add the milk, reduce the heat to low, cover the skillet, and simmer very gently until the fish is very tender, about 1½ hours. Care must be taken to cook the fish gently in order to ensure that the pieces remain whole.

Keep a close eye on the salt cod as it cooks, slipping a spatula now and then under each piece to prevent it from sticking while simultaneously not disturbing it too much. Serve immediately with hot, loose polenta.

Note: *Baccalà alla vicentina* can also be baked. Proceed as directed, but in place of an ample skillet, use an ample, heavy-bottomed ovenproof casserole dish that can also be used on the stove top. Once you have added the milk, slide the dish into an oven preheated to 300 degrees F and bake until the fish is very tender, about 1½ hours.

BUYING *BACCALÀ*

Once, it was impossible to find baccalà, *or salt cod, in the United States outside of the Italian and Hispanic neighborhoods of big cities. It is heartening to see it in mainstream food markets now, but unfortunately the most common type is refrigerated salt cod neatly packaged on Styrofoam trays covered with plastic wrap, and it is not of good quality. Because it is is preserved with less salt than in the traditional method, the flesh of the dehydrated fish is flabby when rehydrated and cooked. This shortcut in processing reduces the soaking time substantially, but compromises the flavor and texture.* Baccalà *preserved the old-fashioned way with more salt (this type is much drier) must be soaked for two days, not one, and the water must be changed once or twice a day.*

Look for genuine, boneless salt cod that is sold loose in stacks, or hangs from hooks in the open-air stalls of ethnic markets. Pick out meaty, white fillets, not thin, dark pieces. It is best to procure boneless and skinless baccalà. *While it is more expensive, is takes far less time to prepare and has less waste.*

The procession led by papà del gnoco *on his donkey
ends in the Piazza San Xeno, where tents serving
gnocchi and* gnocchetti *(little gnocchi) to all
the carnival-goers are set up all around the open
square. This is the same square where the Goth king
Theodoric defeated the barbarian armies of
Odoacre in battle in* A.D. *489, winning for Verona
its sovereignty. The king gave the Veronese the
legions of Odoacre's dead horses, which the citizens
quickly butchered and marinated in wine for
many days. The result was* pastissada, *a sauce of
horse meat, carrots, abundant onion, and the
beautiful Valpolicella wine of Verona (from which
evolved the noble Amarone). Giorgio Gioco,
Verona's most outspoken gastronome, celebrated
chef, and restaurateur, describes gnocchi with one
word:* veronesissimi—"very, very Veronese."
*So passionate are the Veronese for gnocchi that a
word has been coined for the aftereffects of the
celebration,* gnoccolonità—*illness from overeating
gnocchi.*

Pastissada

pastissada de caval

FOR 4 PEOPLE

3 tablespoons unsalted butter

2 tablespoons extra-virgin olive oil

4 ounces pancetta or salt pork,
finely chopped

1 large clove garlic, minced

1 onion, chopped

1 large carrot, peeled and chopped

1 celery stalk, including leaves, chopped

1 bay leaf

scant $1/2$ teaspoon ground coriander

$1/4$ teaspoon ground cloves

$1 1/2$ pounds ground beef or venison

8 ounces chicken giblets, trimmed of fat,
membranes, and any discoloration, chopped

$2/3$ cup dry red wine, preferably Amarone,
or dry white wine, preferably Soave

3 tablespoons tomato paste

$3 1/2$ cups peeled, seeded, and chopped
fresh or canned plum tomatoes

1 teaspoon sea salt

freshly ground white or black pepper

Basic Polenta (page 92)

*Horse meat is the traditional meat used for this dish. I make it with
beef, and it is very good. There are many of ways of making this
famous dish. An old recipe I came across called for sixteen or more
hours of gentle cooking. Others prescribe cooking only as long
as necessary for the meat to become tender and marry with the other
flavors, about 1 ½ hours. This version is essentially a ragù, while
in other recipes, the meat is cooked whole, then shredded into
the sauce after cooking. The meat also may be diced or cubed, which
results in a stew. Pastissada is typically served with potato gnocchi
(page 68) in Verona, where it is the dish of honor at Verona's
Venerdì Gnoccolare (page 154). It is an old tradition in Venice to
sauce the city's bigoli with it. Just as often, pastissada tops polenta,
either in its loose form or grilled.*

In a large saucepan, warm the butter with the oil over
medium-low heat. When they are hot, add the pancetta
and sauté until golden, 7 to 9 minutes. Add the garlic,
onion, carrot, celery, bay leaf, coriander, and cloves and
sauté over low heat until the vegetables are well softened,
12 to 15 minutes. Add the ground meat and the giblets,
using a wooden spoon to break them up. Turn the meats
over to brown evenly, cooking until lightly colored,
5 to 7 minutes. Now add the wine and allow the alcohol to
evaporate, about 3 minutes. Stir in the tomato paste
and sauté gently for 2 to 3 minutes, then add the chopped
tomatoes and salt. Cover partially and simmer over low
heat, stirring occasionally, until the sauce thickens
and is aromatic, about 1½ hours. If it seems to be drying
out, add a few tablespoons of water to moisten. Add pepper
to taste and remove the bay leaf.

Pour the hot, loose polenta into a large, shallow serving
dish. Use the back of a large spoon to create a well
in the center. Spoon the meat mixture atop the polenta.
Serve immediately.

Lagoon Shrimp with Polenta

schie agio e ogio con polenta

FOR 4 PEOPLE

1 1/2 pounds small shrimp in the shell

1 tablespoon kosher salt

3 1/2 tablespoons extra-virgin olive oil

1 clove garlic, finely minced or passed through a garlic press

2 tablespoons chopped fresh Italian parsley

Basic Polenta (page 92)

 Unlike the larger Adriatic shrimp known as conòce *in the local dialect,* schie *are tiny, and almost transparent when uncooked. In the traditional Venetian kitchen, they are most often fried and eaten with polenta. One Venetian, Maurizio Pellegrin, described* schie agio e ogio *to me as so delicious that, he said, while gesticulating dramatically, "I could throw myself out the window with ecstasy every time I eat them." Flavia, my quick-witted friend, replied, "It's easy for you to say that, you live in Venice, and when you throw yourself out the window, you just go for a swim in the Grand Canal."*

These succulent little shrimp are so good in part because they are fresh from the day's catch when eaten in true Venetian style. For non-Venetians who are not blessed with schie, *other varieties of very fresh, small shrimp will have to do.* Schie agio e ogio *are sometimes served with hot, creamy polenta in Venice, or on their own as an antipasto.*

In Venice, a fine restaurant rendition of this famous dish can be found at Antiche Carampane at the foot of the Ponte due Tetti (Bridge of the Two Breasts) (page 148).

Rinse the shrimp in cold running water and drain well. Fill a large saucepan with 4 quarts of water and bring to a rapid boil. Slip the shrimp and the salt into the pan and cover immediately so that the water returns to the boil as quickly as possible. The moment the shrimp turn pink, after 2 or 3 minutes, drain them in a colander. Using a paring knife, remove the shell and the dark intestinal vein that runs down the back of each shrimp, and rinse quickly in cool running water to wash off any traces of the intestinal matter. Drain thoroughly and slice each shrimp in half lengthwise, cutting along the line left by the deveining.

Place the shrimp in a serving bowl with the olive oil, garlic, and parsley and toss all together. Check for seasoning and serve immediately with hot, loose polenta.

Red Beans with Pancetta, Cloves, Rosemary, and Wine in the Style of Venice

fasoi in potacin

FOR 6 TO 8 PEOPLE

6 cups undrained cooked Lamon beans (page 32) or canned beans (see recipe introduction)

2 tablespoons unsalted butter

$1/4$ cup extra-virgin olive oil

2 bay leaves

8 whole cloves

2 ounces lean pancetta or 1 ounce salt pork, chopped

1 onion, finely chopped

1 large carrot, peeled and finely chopped

1 large celery stalk, including leaves, finely chopped

2 small hot red chilies

2 fresh rosemary sprigs, each 4 to 6 inches long, or 1 teaspoon crumbled dried rosemary

2 fresh or canned plum tomatoes, peeled, seeded, and chopped (optional)

$1/2$ cup dry white wine

$1^1/2$ teaspoons sea salt

Basic Polenta (page 92)

 The red beans of Lamon are used for this interesting dish from the Adria area in the Veneto. Dried or canned kidney or cranberry beans, may be substituted with very good results. Keep in mind that dried beans that are kept too long on the shelf—that of the grocer or the cook—become too hard to rehydrate, no matter how long the cooking time.

In traditional bean dishes from the Veneto, tomato paste or tomatoes are not typically added, as the use of tomatoes in cooking was not common in the north until after World War II. Thus, the addition of a little tomato is a relatively modern touch. I like to use it for color and the extra body it contributes to the sauce.

Strain both the home-cooked beans and the canned beans and reserve the liquid. In an ample skillet, warm the butter and the olive oil over medium-low heat. Add the bay leaves, cloves, pancetta, onion, carrot, celery, chilies, and rosemary and sauté until the vegetables are softened, 12 to 15 minutes. Add the tomatoes, if using, and stir to combine. Stir in the beans and a cup or more of their liquid. Simmer the beans very gently over low heat until an aromatic, creamy liquid results, 20 to 30 minutes. If the beans are not almost soupy with abundant liquid, add more of the bean liquid from the beans and continue to simmer until the desired consistency is achieved. Stir in the wine and salt and simmer for another 5 minutes to evaporate the alcohol and blend the flavors.

If you have used fresh rosemary sprigs, fish them out and discard. Serve the beans alongside hot, loose polenta.

5

Second Courses with Fish and Meat

*The Grand Canal as
seen from Ca' Franchetti .*

Venetian cooks are sometimes prone to elaborate fish a bit more than cooks in most other Italian regions, where a scrap of parsley and good olive oil usually suffice. Bass, sole, monkfish, or the prized *San Pietro* (John Dory in English) may be grilled and topped with sautéed radicchio or baby artichoke hearts when they are in season. Typical are fresh anchovies "cooked" in citrus juices or marinated in caper sauce, along with gilt head, bream, eel, red and gray mullet, and turbot, which are pickled, sauced, and pampered. In Chioggia, the fishing capital of the region, a tasty lagoon fish called *gò* (for *ghiozza*, or *gobbius* in Latin) is worked into a brothy risotto, a dish that was once cooked aboard fishing boats for a one-pot meal. A Venetian fish fry is often a glorious crispy, golden pile of soft-shelled crabs, fresh sardines, clams, squid, prawns, and monkfish, with crisp grilled polenta slices on the side.

Freshwater fish is plentiful throughout the Veneto, rich as it is in rivers, streams, and lakes. A cult of fish exists around Lake Garda, the great size and depths of which support tremendous variety, including trout, tench, perch, bass, and crayfish. *Carpione del Garda*, carp from Lake Garda, is particularly esteemed for its refined and delicate texture and delicious flavor. In past times, its numbers were protected by the Republic of Venice through a ducal decree, and it was the highlight of banquets in royal and wealthy households. Good, casual fish restaurants are plentiful in Bardolino and the other towns scattered on the lakeshore.

As for meat, the Venetians can generally do without it, except for pork and all its possibilities. *Che te possa morir el mascio* (Your pig should die), is a Venetian expression that was once among the worst curses that could be hurled at someone. It wasn't everyone who had the means to raise a pig. Whoever did considered the animal a great resource because it fed an entire family for a year. The slaughter was a ritual that took place in mid-December, so that fresh meat was available for Christmas, New Year's Day, and the Epiphany, while the balance was made into hams, sausages, and other cured meats for the rest of the year. The value of the pig, as a Belluno restaurateur told me, is that every part of the animal was utilized for food except for its toenails. Of course, the aristocracy always had access to meat, an observation verified by a piece of Venetian advice passed along by English author Norman Douglas: "A piece of loin pork simmered in milk is a good restorative."

Venetians are influenced by the East in some of their meat cookery. *Agrodolce* (sweet-and-sour) marinades and sauces persist, for example, or a sweet flavor may turn up alongside a savory one. During my childhood, my mother, who had lived with a Venetian family in Rome during the war, told stories about the kinds of foods they ate, many of them exotic and elaborate in comparison to the cooking of Rome and Sardinia, which was all she knew then. Like her, the family had fled their native regions. She talked about the extravagant use of raw ingredients, treasures the family's cook managed to acquire on the black market in order to satisfy the master of the house. She couldn't bear the combination of calves' livers with sultanas and pine nuts, a Venetian specialty. Eventually, the cook began to make something else just for her when liver was on the menu.

Finally the people of the Veneto are also fond of game. Venice and its surrounding islands are essentially marshland. One has only to remember Ernest Hemingway's escapades in Torcello, where he loved to hunt—and where he is said to have decimated the entire duck population. The mainland pursues game, too, but nowhere is it more coveted than in the mountain region of Belluno. Particularly prized there for eating is *capriolo*, the tasty flesh of roe deer that feed on the wild herbs of the hillsides.

I have a very capable young woman from Thailand working in my kitchen. Sometimes she cooks Thai specialties for our family because we always like to try new things. She made a delicious soup the other day, but the problem was that she bought the chicken from the butcher. I had to eat it to be polite, but I can't stomach chicken that I don't raise myself.

—Salvatore Manzi, proprietor,
Le Garzette Azienda Agrituristica

Mullets in the Manner
of Murano

triglie alla muranese

FOR 4 PEOPLE

4 mullets (about 1 ^{1}/$_2$ pounds each), cleaned

sea salt

8 bay leaves

extra-virgin olive oil

^{1}/$_2$ cup white wine vinegar

freshly ground white pepper

 Mullet is uncommon in American fish markets, but it is worth seeking out. The fish are coral or gray and have delicate white flesh that is exceptionally tasty. In this recipe, bay imparts a rich and strong perfume. Venetians, who are experts in fish cookery, know how to cook this fish without first gutting it, which delivers its flavor to the maximum. Novices are advised to scale and gut the fish as thoroughly as any other before cooking it. Serve with slices of grilled polenta (page 92), drizzled with extra-virgin olive oil.

Preheat the broiler. Alternatively, if cooking on an outdoor grill, prepare a fire and permit the wood or coals to burn to a white heat. If cooking in a broiler, you will want to place the fish on a preheated rack over a roasting pan so that the heat can circulate on all sides of the fish as it cooks. If cooking over an open fire, you will want to place the fish between two racks, or in a fish "cage," so that they may be turned over easily and without breaking midway through cooking.

Rinse the fish and dry well with paper towels. Lightly sprinkle the cavity of each fish with salt, then stuff 2 bay leaves into each cavity. Massage olive oil liberally on both sides of the fish, then sprinkle on half of the vinegar.

If broiling, place the fish on the preheated broiling pan about 5 inches under the heat source. Leave the oven door ajar and cook until the fish are golden and crisp on the outside, about 10 minutes. Remove the pan from the broiler, turn the fish over, sprinkle with the remaining vinegar, and slide the pan under the broiler again. Cook for an additional 8 minutes. If cooking over a wood fire, flip over the fish in the racks or cage when the skins crisp and cook on the reverse side until done, a total of about 15 minutes. When done, the fish should be opaque throughout when tested with the tip of a knife, and golden on the surface.

Season the fish with salt and pepper. Serve at once.

Luca Fasoli's Carp
Braised in Beer

carpa alla birra

FOR 4 PEOPLE

1 carp (5$^1/_2$ pounds), cleaned

4 tablespoons ($^1/_2$ stick) unsalted butter

1 large onion, quartered and thinly sliced

1 celery stalk, julienned

1 carrot, peeled and julienned

sea salt

freshly ground white or black pepper

1 bay leaf

1 small bunch fresh Italian parsley, tied with kitchen string

1 bottle (12 ounces) beer

I met Luca Fasoli in Bardolino when he was a student at the hotel school there. He was creating a compendium of fish recipes from the lake district, which included this lovely recipe for carp. I didn't think much about carp before I came across it in Umbria and the Veneto, but it overshadows other freshwater fish in flavor. Around the Garda district, it is enormously popular. The beer bath for the fish was a new idea to me, but the result is splendid. A fish poacher of adequate size, with a lifting tray insert, is necessary for keeping the fish whole during cooking.

Bring the fish to room temperature. Preheat the oven to 350 degrees F.

In an ample skillet, melt 3 tablespoons of the butter over medium-low heat. Add the onion, celery, and carrot and sauté until they soften and color nicely, about 10 minutes.

While the vegetables are sautéing, rinse the fish thoroughly inside and out. Sprinkle the cavity with salt and pepper and place the bay leaf and parsley inside.

Select a fish poacher of appropriate size. It should not be overly large. Butter the tray insert and place the carp on it; lower the tray into the poacher. Cover the fish with the sautéed vegetables and pour the beer over all. Cover the poacher and place it in the oven. Bake until the fish is opaque throughout when tested with the tip of a knife. Cooking time will be 6 minutes to the pound, or about 35 minutes total.

Remove the poacher from the oven, uncover, and immediately lift the fish out of the cooking liquid. Peel off the thick skin and remove the parsley and bay leaf from the cavity. Take care not to break up the fish. Transfer the fish to a warmed serving platter. Melt the remaining 1 tablespoon butter and drizzle over the fish. Strain the hot cooking liquid through a fine-mesh sieve, reserving the vegetables and some liquid. Use the liquid to moisten the surface of the fish, then garnish the fish with the cooked vegetables. Serve immediately.

Remi's Sea Scallops
with Goose Prosciutto

capesante al ristorante Remi

FOR 4 PEOPLE

3 fennel bulbs

$^{1}/_{2}$ onion

16 jumbo sea scallops

$^{3}/_{4}$ cup extra-virgin olive oil

1 teaspoon ground fennel seed

2 ounces smoked goose prosciutto (see recipe introduction), cut into tiny pieces

1 cup dry white wine

1 tablespoon unsalted butter

sea salt

freshly ground white or black pepper

$^{1}/_{4}$ cup unbleached flour

I was treated to this splendid dish by Francesco Antonucci, owner of Remi, New York City's celebrated Venetian restaurant. Remi is among the few places outside of Venice where traditional Venetian dishes can be found, but, as every inspired chef does, Francesco often creates interpretations of classic dishes. Goose prosciutto can be purchased in many specialty-food shops or by mail order (page 158). Unlike pork prosciutto, which is air-cured, goose "prosciutto" is smoked. Its flavor gives a lively boost to this dish.

Trim the fronds, stalks, and tough core from each fennel bulb, then halve the bulbs lengthwise. Cut them into julienne. Cut the onion into julienne of equal size.

Rinse the scallops under cold running water and dry thoroughly with paper towels. Set aside.

In an ample, heavy-bottomed skillet, warm ¼ cup of the olive oil over medium heat. Add the julienned fennel and sauté, tossing occasionally, until tender, 8 to 10 minutes. Transfer to a bowl. Rinse out the skillet and set aside.

In a heavy-bottomed pot or Dutch oven, warm ¼ cup of the olive oil over medium heat. When it is sizzling hot, add the onion, ground fennel, and goose prosciutto and sauté until the onion is wilted, about 3 minutes. Add the cooked fennel and toss. Pour in the wine and simmer until the alcohol evaporates, about 3 minutes. Remove from the heat, stir in the butter and salt and pepper to taste, and toss until the butter melts evenly. Set aside.

In the skillet used for cooking the fennel, warm the remaining ¼ cup olive oil over medium heat. Spread the flour on a plate. Dredge the scallops in the flour, shaking off the excess flour, and slip them immediately into the hot oil. (To ensure a crispy coating, it is important not to permit the flour-coated scallops to rest before they are sautéed.) Sauté the scallops until they are browned all over, 4 to 5 minutes. The scallops should be neither raw in the center nor overcooked. Use a slotted spoon to transfer them to a plate lined with paper towels.

Arrange the fennel and onion mixture on 4 dinner plates. Place 4 scallops over each. Serve immediately.

Rabbit in the Old Style

coniglio alla vecchia maniera

FOR 4 PEOPLE

1 rabbit (2$\frac{1}{2}$ pounds), cut into serving pieces

1 tablespoon kosher salt

freshly ground coarse black pepper

5 large cloves garlic, minced

6 tablespoons extra-virgin olive oil

sea salt

This recipe is adapted from Ricette di osterie del Veneto: quaresime e oriente, *by Luisa Bellina and Mimmo Cappellaro, a delightful collection of recipes taken from osterie in the Veneto. The use of rabbit in the kitchen is widespread throughout the region. In this uncomplicated, succulent dish, the meat is permeated with the flavor of garlic and pepper.*

Rinse the rabbit pieces under cold running water, then leave them to soak in cold water to cover and the kosher salt for about 1 hour. Drain, rinse in cold water, and dry well with paper towels.

Preheat the oven to 300 degrees F. Select a baking dish with a tight-fitting lid large enough to accommodate the rabbit pieces without crowding and generously oil it. Place the rabbit in the dish and sprinkle lavishly with pepper. Strew the garlic over the rabbit, then drizzle evenly with the olive oil.

Position the lid tightly on top and slide the dish into the oven. Bake until the rabbit is tender, a total of 2 hours. Turn the rabbit pieces over after 1 hour and sprinkle them with some sea salt after 1$\frac{1}{2}$ hours. Transfer the rabbit and any juices to a warmed platter and serve immediately.

POMEGRANATES

Pomegranates are in season in late autumn
through early winter. For the best flavor, select
fruits that are large and vibrantly colored. The
outer skin is naturally somewhat tight and
leathery, but it should be taut, thin, and resilient
to the touch, not tough, wrinkled, and dried
out. Look for pomegranate juice in health-food
stores and Middle Eastern markets. To inten-
sify the flavor of the juice, simmer it to evaporate
the liquid by about one third.

*In order to give good flavor to young fowl, take
a pomegranate and make wine with it by
hand, and put in that wine good sweet spices, and
if it seems too strong, put more, otherwise [add]
rose water....*

—FROM A FOURTEENTH-CENTURY RECIPE

Roast Young Hen Turkey
with Pomegranate Sauce

tacchinella arrostita al melograno

FOR 8 PEOPLE

1 young hen turkey (5 to 7 pounds)

3 tablespoons unsalted butter, melted, and mixed with 2 tablespoons extra-virgin olive oil

sea salt

freshly ground black pepper

large handful of fresh sage leaves with stems intact

1 large onion, cut into 8 wedges

3 cups bottled pomegranate juice

1 pomegranate

2 tablespoons *vin santo* or port (optional)

 Quando a novembre el vin no xe più mosto, la paèta xe pronta per el rosto! *(When in November the wine is no longer must, the young turkey is ready for the roasting!)*

This old adage from Vicenza signaled the beginning of the season for cooking turkey with pomegranate juice, one of the most sumptuous dishes of the Vicenza kitchen. The "sacrifice" of the young bird traditionally takes place on November 11, the day that marks the end of the harvest and the maturation of the pomegranate.

The female turkey is more tender and tastier than the tom. An independent butcher can usually special-order hen turkeys weighing between 5 and 7 pounds. If a larger bird is used, adjust the ingredients proportionately and lengthen the cooking time.

Bring the turkey to room temperature before preparing it for cooking. Preheat the oven to 325 degrees F.

Rinse the turkey thoroughly and dry it well inside and out with paper towels. Massage both cavities of the bird with some of the butter–olive oil mixture, then sprinkle with salt and pepper. Stuff sage leaves and onion wedges into both cavities. Sew the cavities closed with kitchen string, then use string to truss the wings and legs close to the body. Rub the bird well all over with the butter-oil mixture and place it on a rack in a roasting pan. The size of the pan should correspond to the size of the bird and should not be more than 2 inches deep. The rack prevents the bird from frying in its own fat.

Slide the pan into the oven. Roast until an instant-read thermometer inserted deep into the thigh alongside the thigh bone registers 160 to 170 degrees F. The internal temperature depends on your preference for well-done

continued

Roast Young Hen Turkey
with Pomegranate Sauce
continued

(170 degrees F) or very juicy with a hint of pale pink (160 degrees F). As a rule of thumb, a 6- to 7-pound turkey will roast in 2 to 2 ¼ hours.

During the first half of the cooking, baste the turkey with the remaining butter-oil mixture and, in time, with its own juices, always remembering to remove the bird from the oven to do so and to shut the oven door immediately after placing the bird on the stove top to baste. Frequent basting— every 10 to 15 minutes—is critical to the flavor and moisture of the bird. Retain moisture by turning the turkey onto alternate sides each time it is basted.

Also during the first half of the roasting, pour the pomegranate juice into a saucepan and simmer over low heat to reduce its volume by one third. When the turkey has cooked halfway, baste it with its own juices and some of the concentrated pomegranate juice.

While the bird roasts, peel the pomegranate fruit. This is a tedious task, but the burst of tart, cool juice from the glistening seeds sprinkled over the tender turkey meat makes it well worth the trouble. Using a sharp paring knife, make a cut in the blossom end of the fruit and peel away the tough outer skin. Once inside, peel away as much of the white membrane, along with the outer skin, as possible, taking care not to pierce the seeds. When much of this has been peeled away, the pomegranate can be gently pried open with the fingers dividing it roughly in half along its natural sections. Now pry apart each of

the halves to produce 4 sections in all. Pull away the remaining white membranes and push the seeds into a bowl with your fingers, taking care not to pierce the seeds and to remove any surrounding white membrane left on them. Cover the bowl and set aside.

When the bird is done, remove it from the oven immediately and transfer it to a carving board. Sprinkle the bird all over with salt, cover it loosely with aluminum foil, and allow it to rest for 20 to 30 minutes. Meanwhile, skim off the fat from the pan drippings and combine them with the remaining concentrated pomegranate juice (the proportion of drippings to pomegranate juice can vary from equal amounts to 2 parts drippings mixed with 1 part pomegranate juice). Simmer to heat the sauce through and adjust the flavor to taste with a little salt. If a slightly sweeter, richer flavor is desired, add the *vin santo* to taste and simmer for a few minutes longer.

Carve the turkey. Serve the sauce laced over the carved portions of the bird on each plate, and scatter the pomegranate seeds on top.

Grilled Duck Breast
with Blueberry Sauce

anatra con salsa di mirtilli

FOR 6 PEOPLE

3 boneless duck breasts (³/₄ pound each)

2 pints fresh or frozen blueberries, rinsed

1 tablespoon freshly squeezed lemon juice

3-inch-long strip lemon zest

1 tablespoon extra-virgin olive oil

sea salt

La Loggia Rambaldi in Bardolino offers this duck dish when the mirtilli, *whortleberries (also called mountain grapes), are in season. The berries grow on aromatic wild shrubs in the Alps and the Apennines. They are pea-size, their color deep blue with a jet cast. Sweet and astringent at once, they are excellent for meat and game sauces. The closest relative of the* mirtillo *in the United States is the blueberry, although it lacks the necessary tang. To compensate for this, I've increased the amount of lemon juice in the original recipe, with quite pleasant results. As for the duck, it is best when cooked on a open wood fire, but it can be broiled indoors.*

Bring the duck breasts to room temperature. Trim any excess fat from the breasts, then pound them lightly to tenderize and flatten.

Prepare a fire in an outdoor grill, using a hardwood such as oak, if possible. The fire is ready when the embers are at their hottest, that is, white and glowing. Arrange them around the edges of the grill to produce indirect heat, leaving a few embers in the center. Transfer the duck breasts to the center of the grill and cook, turning occasionally, until the skin is nicely colored and crisp and the meat juices run clear when tested with the tip of a knife, about 30 minutes.

Meanwhile, in a saucepan, combine the berries, lemon juice, and lemon zest over medium-low heat. Cook until the berries disintegrate into a thick compote, about 20 minutes. Let cool somewhat, remove the zest and discard, and pass the berries through a food mill, or purée them in a food processor. Reheat before serving, remove from the stove, and stir in the olive oil.

When the duck breasts are done, transfer them to a cutting board that will collect the meat's natural juices; let rest for 10 minutes. Sprinkle with salt to taste. Cut into thin slices on the diagonal and transfer the slices to a serving platter. Pour the natural juices over the meat, then spoon some of the sauce over it. Serve, passing the remaining sauce at the table.

Roasted Guinea Fowl
with Peverada Sauce

faraona con salsa peverada

FOR 4 PEOPLE

2 guinea fowl (about 2 pounds each)

sea salt

freshly ground black pepper

$^1/_4$ cup extra-virgin olive oil

2 ounces pancetta, chopped

8 fresh sage leaves or 1 teaspoon crumbled
dried sage

2 fresh rosemary sprigs or 1 teaspoon
crumbled dried rosemary

$^1/_2$ cup dry white wine

1 cup water, homemade meat broth,
or good-quality chicken broth

Peverada Sauce (page 42)

 Salsa peverada, *a mixture of livers,* anchovies,
bread crumbs, soppressata, *and seasonings,*
was a favorite of the Venetian aristocracy, who
primarily paired it with roasted game. Nowadays,
it is commonly matched with guinea fowl, of
which Italians are inordinately fond. Called pintelle
in French, a guinea fowl is more subtle in flavor
than a turkey, more tasty than a chicken, and more
meaty than a duck (see mail-order sources, page
158). Because the meat is low in fat, it is best to
roast the birds in a pan on the stove top, rather than
cook them in the dry heat of an oven. Delicate
and tasty, they are fitting birds to carry the elegant
peverada *sauce.*

Rinse the birds thoroughly and dry well inside and out
with paper towels. Lightly sprinkle the cavities with salt
and pepper. Sew the cavities closed with kitchen string.

Select a Dutch oven or other heavy-bottomed pot that
is large enough to hold the 2 birds without crowding them
and warm the olive over medium-high heat. Add the
pancetta, sage, rosemary, and the birds, reduce the heat
to medium, and sauté until the birds are browned on
all sides, about 10 minutes. Use tongs to turn the birds to
avoid punctures that cause juices to escape. Add the wine
and cook for 3 minutes to allow the alcohol to evaporate.

Set the birds on their backs. Add salt to taste and $^1/_2$ cup
of the water, cover partially, and bring to a simmer.
Reduce the temperature to low and cook, partially covered,
until the birds are tender, about $1^1/_4$ hours. Add water,
a few tablespoons at a time, as necessary to prevent the
birds and vegetables from drying out, but do not turn
the birds. To test for doneness, make a cut in the leg joint
to see if the juices run clear. If not, continue to cook
until tender, 10 to 15 minutes more. Do not overcook; the
hens have a very low fat content and will dry out easily.
Remove the pot from the heat and remove birds from the
pot. Cover them loosely with foil and allow to rest for
15 to 20 minutes.

Skim the fat off the pan drippings and reheat the drippings.
Cut the birds in half laterally and remove the trussing
thread. Transfer to a serving platter and top the pieces with
the peverada sauce. Pass any additional drippings at the
table. Serve immediately.

Pork Ribs with Sauerkraut and Polenta

costine di maiale con crauti e polenta

FOR 4 PEOPLE

3¹/₂ pounds smoked or fresh pork ribs
(bone-in rib ends or country ribs),
cut off the rib section into individual ribs

5 tablespoons extra-virgin olive oil

3 cloves garlic, minced

1 tablespoon fresh rosemary, minced,
or 1 teaspoon crumbled dried rosemary

1 tablespoon fresh sage, minced,
or 1 teaspoon crumbled dried sage

¹/₂ teaspoon ground juniper berries

1 cup dry white wine

¹/₂ cup water

³/₄ teaspoon sea salt

¹/₄ teaspoon freshly ground black pepper

1 large onion, sliced

1 ounce smoked ham, sliced and then
chopped

1 pound sauerkraut, rinsed

Grilled Polenta (page 92)

This is an adaptation of a dish from the Belluno Province. There, the legs and neck of the pig are always designated for hams, sausages, and salamis. While ribs are traditionally smoked over juniper wood, I have revised the recipe for use with fresh pork ribs. Costine are the meaty ribs from the shoulder, often labeled "country ribs" in American markets. The ribs cook gently in wine for a long time, which renders them fork-tender.

Trim any excess fat from the ribs. In an ample, heavy-bottomed skillet, warm 3 tablespoons of the the olive oil. Add the ribs and sauté on all sides until nicely browned, about 8 minutes total. Remove the meat from the skillet and transfer to a plate. Add another tablespoon of the olive oil to the pan. Add the garlic, rosemary, sage, and juniper and sauté over gentle heat for 1 minute. Add the wine and the water and stir. Simmer to evaporate, about 2 minutes. Return the ribs to the skillet and add the salt and pepper; cover tightly. Simmer over the gentlest possible heat until tender, about 1¹/₂ hours.

About 15 minutes before the meat is cooked, in a separate skillet, warm the remaining tablespoon of olive oil over low heat. Add the onion and smoked ham and sauté, stirring occasionally, until soft and translucent, about 3 minutes. Stir in the sauerkraut and sauté for about 2 minutes to heat through. Transfer to a large serving platter.

When the ribs are ready, transfer them to the bed of sauerkraut. There should be about 1¹/₄ cups meat juices in the pan. If there is less, add water to the skillet, up to ¹/₄ cup, and bring to a boil. Strain the juices through a fine-mesh sieve and pour over the meat. Serve the ribs and the sauerkraut with slices of grilled polenta.

6

contorni

Vegetable Side Dishes

Preparing broad beans

One summer when I was convalescing after an illness, I decided to visit Venice. If I hadn't known about Le Garzette Azienda Agrituristica, an intimate farm and inn on the Lido, Venice, with all its allure, would have been last on my list of places to go. The inn was set close to both coasts of the narrow island, the lagoon on the east, and the open sea on the west. My daughters only needed to unlatch an old wooden gate behind the vineyard and scramble up a short incline to find themselves on a white sandy beach where goatherds passed several times a day with their flocks. At day's end, from our balcony, we would watch the shining night view of the lagoon, the ferries with their distant red lights making beelines for Venice, so silent and effortless from where we stood.

Salvatore, an expatriate Neapolitan, and his Venetian wife, Renza, had bought the place some years before and turned it into a working farm. Salvatore's domain was the gardens, the hen-house, and the vineyards, all of which he tended himself. Renza's sphere was the kitchen, which she ran with great precision, always conscious of what the cycle of the seasons would provide.

It was June, just in time for pumpkin flowers, green beans, squashes, and eggplants. The flowers were batter-fried or cut into ribbons and sautéed in good olive oil, with onion and the leaves of young field poppies, to combine with pasta or risotto. The beans were picked young, so that they were velvety and sweet when cooked. The eggplants went from field to table within a day, so their seeds had no time to become bitter. Renza dipped rounds of the narrow eggplants in batter and fried them to a golden crisp. My little daughter, who had always refused to eat eggplant before, called them "the cookie things." An imaginary line had to be drawn down the center of the serving platter, and "cookie things" apportioned equally on each side to prevent battles between the children for the biggest ones. The meal often consisted entirely of vegetables, from the antipasto through the first, second, and side-dish courses.

During the weeks we spent there, I became stronger and stronger from the vegetable meals set before me. Part of the therapy was the pleasure of watching the harvesting rituals. Our rooms overlooked the courtyard outside the kitchen entrance where the family gathered to prepare the vegetables Salvatore brought in from the fields. We watched them nip bean stems and peel artichokes, as their soft Venetian chatter drifted just below us. So we began our mornings on our balcony, just as we ended our evenings there, watching the comings, the goings, and the constants amid the vegetable fields, all the while under the sunshine and the moonlight that lit Venice, too. We boarded the *traghetto* for Venice every day, and Gabriella and Celina had seen something of La Serenissima in between our meals at the inn. But only the mildest regrets entered my thoughts that here we were in Venice and we hadn't seen enough of her.

Indeed, it was no worse than every other visit when I came away, as Henry James had said he had done, feeling that he had gleaned only the flimsiest knowledge of her treasures and the most superficial insight into her character. No, it was better this time, much better, on this balcony between the lagoon and the sea, looking out at the vegetable garden that I had borrowed.

Co riva el 30 de agosto
tute le suche le va a rosto!

When August 30 arrives
all of the pumpkins should
be roasted!

Sweet-and-Sour Carrots

carote in agrodolce

FOR 6 PEOPLE

$^1/_2$ cup sultanas

$^1/_2$ cup sweet Marsala, or as needed

2 pounds young carrots, peeled

3 tablespoons unsalted butter, olive oil, or a combination

3 tablespoons water

$^1/_4$ teaspoon sea salt

$^1/_4$ cup pine nuts, lightly toasted

finely grated zest of 1 orange

1 tablespoon white wine vinegar

 I have come across many interesting recipes in the Venetian-Jewish tradition, such as this one, which elevates carrots to a high level. The combining of sweet and savory is a major theme in Jewish cooking. A photograph of this recipe appears on page 109.

La Salute, Venice

In a small bowl, combine the sultanas with Marsala to cover. Allow to soak for an hour or so. Slice the carrots into $^1/_2$-inch-thick disks, or into the same thickness first horizontally and then on the diagonal for an oval shape.

In an ample, heavy-bottomed skillet, warm the butter over medium-low heat. Add the carrots and water, cover tightly, reduce the heat to low, and cook, stirring occasionally with a wooden spoon to ensure even cooking, until the carrots are tender but still somewhat resistant to the bite, 10 to 12 minutes. If necessary, add an additional tablespoon or two of water occasionally to prevent the carrots from drying out, burning, or sticking to the bottom of the pan. When the carrots are half cooked, uncover and add the salt, sultanas and Marsala, pine nuts, orange zest, and vinegar. Check for salt and serve promptly.

Asparagus with
Hard-Cooked Eggs

asparagi all'Azienda Le Garzette

FOR 4 PEOPLE

3 very fresh eggs, preferably organic

1 pound asparagus

1 teaspoon kosher salt

extra-virgin olive oil

freshly ground white pepper

sea salt

The Veneti put asparagus and eggs together in many ways. The simplest of all is arranging hard-cooked eggs and cooked asparagus together in a contorno. At Le Garzette Azienda Agrituristica, a lovely inn on Venice's famed Lido, the asparagus is pulled out of the ground only hours before it is cooked for you, and the eggs are collected from the chickens even as you eat. Only when the ingredients are as fresh as this, moistened with the fragrant olive oil of Lake Garda and washed down with wine from grapes with the memory of the sea upon them, do you realize what a blissful marriage this dish is.

A word of advice: Do not be tempted to steam the asparagus. Its sugar and vivid color are intensified only when it is boiled in salted water.

Place the eggs in a saucepan with cold water to cover and bring to a boil over medium-low heat. Cook for 15 minutes from the time they are placed on the stove. Drain the eggs, rinse with cold water to arrest cooking, and peel them while they are still warm so that they will slip out of their shells easily. Allow them to cool before cutting them, but do not refrigerate them.

Trim the hard bottoms off of the asparagus. Using a paring knife, peel off the thicker skin at the base of each stalk. (By paring away the thicker bottom skin, much of the stalk, which is tender under the tougher lower skin, is saved.) In a skillet large enough to accommodate comfortably the length of the asparagus, bring enough water to cover the asparagus to a boil. First add the kosher salt, then slip in the asparagus, arranging them so that their stems, rather than their tips, are completely immersed. Boil them until they are tender but not mushy, about 6 minutes, depending on how fresh they are. Asparagus should not be undercooked and crisp, nor should they be mushy. Drain them immediately, taking care not to break the tips. Plunge them in cold water to arrest cooking. Immediately drain them thoroughly and transfer them to a platter.

Slice the eggs lengthwise into quarters and arrange them on the platter with the asparagus. Moisten the asparagus and the eggs liberally with olive oil and sprinkle with pepper and sea salt. Serve at room temperature.

One afternoon while I was having pranzo on the
veranda with my companions Paolo and Ester,
we saw Salvatore pass by on his way to the chicken
coop. He was holding the hand of a little golden-
haired boy who, moments before, had been sitting at
a table near ours, having Sunday lunch with his
family. In his other hand, Salvatore held the handle
of a large basket woven from reeds. The eager
child asked, "Signore, where are we going to get the
eggs?" Salvatore replied, "We're going to go to
the hens and get their eggs. Then we will go to the
roosters and see if they have laid any, and we'll take
those as well!" I laughed, but Ester, sitting across
the table from me, seemed lost in thought. She
hadn't heard the conversation, but only the sounds
of the voices. Suddenly, she looked up and said,
"Do you know what Pablo Neruda said about
the Italian language? He said that Italian spoken
by children is like the sound of angels' voices."

—LE GARZETTE AZIENDA AGRITURISTICA,
VENICE-MALAMOCCO, 1998

Braised Artichokes
with Garlic and Parsley

carciofi trifolati

FOR 2 OR 3 PEOPLE

juice of $1/2$ lemon

3 large artichokes (about 8 ounces each)

1 tablespoon extra-virgin olive oil

1 large clove garlic, finely chopped

1 tablespoon chopped fresh Italian parsley

$1/2$ teaspoon chopped fresh marjoram
or $1/4$ teaspoon crumbled dried marjoram

$1/2$ cup water

$1/2$ teaspoon sea salt

freshly ground white or black pepper

At the market at the Piazza delle Erbe in Verona,
I passed an old woman seated on a folding
chair outside her booth. She was peeling artichokes
and throwing their hearts into a pail full of water
with lemon slices. I asked her what she planned to
do with them. "Trifolata, of course," she said,
without looking up. It is the most typical way of
cooking artichokes throughout the Veneto and in
other parts of Italy as well.

Add water to a depth of about 4 inches to a glass bowl (do not use metal), then add the lemon juice. Trim only a thin slice from the bottom of the stem of each artichoke to remove the dark skin. Pare off all the dark green skin on the stem. Pull off the tough outer leaves until you reach leaves that have tender, white areas at their base. Using a serrated knife, cut off the upper, dark green part of the inner leaves; leave the light greenish yellow base. The inner rows of leaves are the tender part you want, so be careful not to cut away too much. Cut each artichoke in half lengthwise and cut out the hairy choke and any other tough inner purple leaves. As each artichoke is finished, immediately put it in the waiting lemon water to prevent it from turning brown. (The artichokes can remain in the lemon water in the refrigerator for up to 24 hours.) When all of the artichokes have been trimmed, drain them and pat dry. Place each artichoke half, cut side down, on a cutting board and cut lengthwise into slices ¼ inch thick.

In a large saucepan, warm the olive oil and garlic over medium heat and sauté until the garlic is softened, 1 to 2 minutes. Add the artichokes, parsley, and marjoram and stir with a wooden spoon to coat the artichokes. Pour in the water and bring to a boil. Add the salt and pepper to taste, reduce the heat to low, cover, and cook until the artichokes are tender, 10 to 15 minutes; the length of time will depend on the freshness of the artichokes. If the artichokes seem to be drying out, add a little water. If you think there is too much liquid once the chokes are half cooked, remove the cover and cook over medium heat until some of it evaporates. Be sure to stir to prevent sticking.

Taste and adjust with salt and pepper. Serve immediately.

Broad Beans Sautéed
with Garlic and Anchovy

cornetti in padella con aglio e alici

FOR 6 PEOPLE

2 pounds young broad beans or green beans, rinsed and ends trimmed

1 tablespoon sea salt

3 tablespoons extra-virgin olive oil

3 large cloves garlic, minced

3 or 4 anchovy fillets packed in olive oil, cut into small pieces

 Unfortunately, broad beans are not easy to find in American markets, but the flat, long, green romano beans, or even regular green beans, may be substituted.

Fill a saucepan with water and bring to a rolling boil. Add the beans and salt. (The salt preserves the bright green color of the beans, so be sure not to leave it out.) Cook until tender, 9 to 10 minutes for broad beans, 7 to 8 minutes for green beans. The beans should be cooked through, tender but not mushy. They should never be crunchy or al dente. In the Italian kitchen, al dente is a cooking treatment reserved primarily for pasta and is not applied to vegetables. To arrive at the sweet, unique flavor of broad beans, cook them until they are as tender as butter is at room temperature. Drain the beans.

In an ample skillet, warm the olive oil and garlic together over medium heat. Sauté until the garlic is softened, about 1 minute. Add the beans and anchovies and toss well to distribute all the ingredients evenly. Serve immediately.

Radicchio Salad with Bacon in the Style of Vicenza

insalata di radicchio alla vicentina

FOR 4 PEOPLE

8 ounces radicchio

1 tablespoon extra-virgin olive oil,
plus more to taste

6 slices lean bacon, preferably nitrite-free,
chopped

sea salt

freshly ground black pepper

$1/2$ cup red or white wine vinegar

This is an adaptation of an old recipe from Vicenza. Traditionally, fresh lard, made by rendering fat back, was heated to a liquid, then vinegar was poured directly into the pan to deglaze it, and the lot was poured over radicchio in a salad bowl. A very tasty dressing was produced by this method. Here, chopped bacon replaces the lard with excellent results. Select a fine vinegar to ensure the best flavor.

Cut the heads of radicchio in half through the stem end. Using a paring knife, remove and discard the core portion on the base of each half. Shred the radicchio into bite-size pieces, then rinse well and dry thoroughly in a salad spinner or by some other method. Place the radicchio in a serving bowl.

In a skillet, warm the 1 tablespoon olive oil over medium heat. Add the bacon and sauté until the bacon bits are nicely colored but not burnt. This should take only a few minutes. Drain off the excess bacon fat and add salt and pepper to taste and the vinegar. Use a wooden spoon to deglaze the skillet, scraping up any bacon bits stuck to the bottom as the vinegar reduces, about 2 minutes. Remove the skillet from the heat and let the bacon cool a bit, then stir in olive oil to taste. Pour the dressing over the salad, using only as much as is needed to coat the radicchio lightly and evenly. Serve at once.

Mauro Stoppa's Sweet-and-Sour Marinated Pumpkin

zucca in saor

FOR 4 PEOPLE

1 small sugar pumpkin, butternut squash, or calabaza (about 2$^1/_2$ pounds)

kosher salt

$^1/_2$ cup unbleached flour

olive oil, safflower oil, or corn oil

1 pound onions, halved or quartered, depending on size, and thinly sliced into half-moons

$^3/_4$ cup sultanas

$^1/_2$ cup white wine vinegar

$^1/_2$ cup sweet white wine, such as Marsala

sea salt

freshly ground black pepper

$^1/_2$ cup pine nuts, lightly toasted

Mauro Stoppa, skipper and cook of the Eolo, which cruises the Venetian lagoon with people aboard lucky enough to find him, gave me his recipe for this traditional Venetian dish. He says that it is the version native to Chioggia, where his ship is docked. Similar recipes are found in the Venetian-Jewish kitchen. While many versions don't call for pine nuts, I can't imagine the dish would be as nice without them. I have taken the liberty of adding sweet white wine to the vinegar in cooking to compensate for the difference in sweetness between the famous zucca of Chioggia and the comparable blandness of American substitutes. There are no extraneous ingredients here; each one adds to a perfect harmony. Of prime importance is that the zucca, or sweet squash that we may have to substitute, be mature, meaty, and sweet, not thin and bland.

Using a sharp knife, cut off the stem and blossom ends from the squash, then halve lengthwise and scoop out and discard the seeds. Cut the halves crosswise into slices ¼ inch to ½ inch thick. Sprinkle the slices lightly with kosher salt, then stand them upright in a colander. Drops of liquid will form on the surface of the slices. Standing them up will allow the liquid to run down and out between the slices when draining, rather than accumulate between horizontal layers. Permit the slices to drain in this fashion for at least 45 minutes or up to several hours.

Use paper towels to wipe off all the salt from the slices. Have ready the flour spread on a plate or on a sheet of waxed paper, and a platter lined with paper towels.

Pour enough oil to cover the squash slices into a large skillet and place over medium-high heat. While the oil is heating, dredge the slices in the flour, shaking off the excess. Once the oil is hot enough to make the squash slices sizzle, slip the slices one at a time into the hot oil.

If the oil begins to cool as a result, turn up the heat a little until the sizzling resumes before adding more slices. Allow plenty of room for each slice so that it can fry to a nice golden brown on both sides; use tongs to turn the slices. The slices should cook in about 12 minutes. Transfer the cooked slices to the towel-lined platter, patting them with more towels to remove excess oil. When all the slices are cooked and drained in this fashion, set them aside, placing them on fresh paper towels if necessary.

Pour all but about 3 tablespoons of the oil from the pan. Reheat the oil over medium-low heat. Add the onions and sauté gently until they are completely softened, lightly colored, and translucent, but not at all brown, about 5 minutes. Stir in the sultanas, vinegar, and wine and continue to cook over medium-low heat until the alcohol evaporates, about 3 minutes. Season with salt and pepper to taste.

Remove the onion mixture from the heat. Select a serving dish that will permit you to arrange the squash slices and onion mixture in 3 layers. Arrange a layer of the slices on the bottom of the dish, cover with one-third of the onion mixture, and sprinkle with one-third of the pine nuts. Repeat two more times.

Cover the dish with plastic wrap and refrigerate for a minimum of 1 day or up to 1 week before serving. Serve at room temperature.

Note: In Mantua, just south of the Veneto, fresh mint is added to sweet-and-sour marinated pumpkin.

7

dolci

Sweets

At the market

The cooks of the Veneto have relied on honey as a sweetener since the time of the Etruscans. *Fugassa de Pasqua*, an Easter bread sweetened with honey that is still made today in the Veneto, appears in a fourth-century mosaic in the basilica of San Marco and is depicted on the table in Leonardo da Vinci's *The Last Supper*.

Honey satisfied the sweet tooth, but its syrupy nature limited its use in cakes and pastries. With the discovery by the Crusaders of cane sugar in the East in the eleventh century, Venetian merchants began to import it for their own use and to sell to other parts of Italy and Europe. Crystallized white sugar made greater refinement in baking possible, and the wealth of the Venetian gentry soon guaranteed its lavish use in the making of confections. One reporter of the times, Giuseppe Maffioli, describes a sculpture made of sugar with the signature of none other than the famous Sansovino at its base. Contemporary author Mariù Salvatori de Zuliani claims that the Venetians invented marzipan in the days when La Serenissima imported vast quantities of almonds from the southern region of Apulia (*marci pane*, they say, or *pan de San Marco*, the "bread of Saint Mark").

The patrician class basked in their sweet luxuries but coexisted with a strong popular tradition of rustic desserts and cookies that could be stored for long periods and that kept well under sail. Among the oldest and most common of these durable cookies are *baìcoli*, which take their name from the little fish of the lagoon that followed the sailors' boats on their long voyages to the Mediterranean during the days of La Serenissima. *Baìcoli* are usually bought rather than baked at home, and they are sold in beautiful tins or exquisite packages everywhere in Venice, from bakeries to general food markets. These and other Venetian cookies, such as *zaletti* (page 143), *bicciolani*, and *busolài*, are hard biscotti designed for dunking in espresso, tea, or hot chocolate. Also among the many sweets of the region are puddings and cakes made of polenta (page 92) or ground chestnuts when they are in season (page 140).

In another category are festive sweets that fill the beautiful window displays of pastry shops in Venice, Verona, and other cities and towns during the carnival season. Part of the merriment of the carnivals that preceded the fast days of Lent was the public feasting and eating of sweets in the *caffè* and on the streets. Fritters of dough or rice and *galàni* (page 144), sweet fried pastries, which have counterparts of varying names all over Italy, are the most prominent of all traditional carnival sweets.

One of the most superb Italian cakes is the light, buttery, and refined *pandoro*, the classic Christmas Eve yeast cake of Verona. This is a cake that in Verona and elsewhere in the Veneto is typically bought from fine bakeries, not made at home. The fine *pandoro* of Verona, in handsome packaging, is exported to specialty-food shops in America during the Christmas season. Another provincial specialty of note is the Belluno region's apple strudel, a close cousin to the Austrian dessert of the same name. Austrian bakers are renowned for their skills and their fine cakes and pastries filled with fruits and poppy seeds, a theme that is repeated in the baking of the eastern half of the alpine region that borders Austria.

As much as the Veneto loves its traditional sweets, it also likes to invent. It is no surprise that it was in Venice, in Arrigo Cipriani's famous Harry's Bar, that tiramisù, the rich Italian trifle of cake layers, mascarpone, cream, and chocolate, was born. The aristocratic and opulent traditions of Venice, combined with the need to cater to an international population of tourists, spur restaurateurs to ever-new dessert creations. In other course categories, this propensity would be gilding the lily. But in the sweet category, there is always room for fantasy.

135

Getting up at four in the morning, going by boat for a dive in the sea, then coming back to Saint Mark's Square, drinking chocolate in my dressing gown, running until one o'clock, coming and going, getting back into my boat until seven, running around by water and land, paying visits until midnight, all the while drinking lemonade, coffee, chocolate, and ice-cream when I am dining alone: this is life in Venice.

—INFINE GROSLEY, EIGHTEENTH CENTURY, BY WAY OF *I menu della seduzione; a tavola con Casanova* (Menus of Seduction: At Table with Casanova)

Pumpkin Pudding Cake

budino di zucca

FOR 4 TO 6 PEOPLE

$^1/_2$ cup sultanas

$^1/_4$ cup grappa or rum

12 amaretti or other plain almond cookies, pulverized

1 small sugar pumpkin or butternut squash (about 2$^3/_4$ pounds)

$^1/_2$ cup, plus 2 tablespoons sugar

$^1/_2$ cup unbleached flour

$^1/_2$ cup milk

3 eggs, separated

1 tablespoon candied ginger or 1 teaspoon peeled and chopped fresh ginger

5 tablespoons pine nuts, lightly toasted and coarsely chopped

$^1/_4$ cup finely sliced, then chopped candied orange peel

pinch of sea salt

scant $^1/_4$ teaspoon cream of tartar

My aunt Annette Messina, a fine baker, took the recipe for budino di zucca *that I brought back from Verona and made it even better. Our pumpkins contain more water than the famous pumpkins of the Veneto, thus the recipe has been adjusted accordingly. Calabaza, cheese pumpkin, and other squashes in this genre may also be used, as long as they do not have a high water content. A solid, moist pudding with the consistency of pumpkin pie, the* budino *is perfumed with the scent of orange, ginger, and grappa or rum. Serve it with espresso or grappa.*

Preheat the oven to 400 degrees F. In a cup or small bowl, combine the sultanas and grappa, and allow to soak until needed. Line a baking sheet with aluminum foil and oil the foil. Generously butter a 9-inch square baking pan and coat it with the pulverized cookies.

Cut the squash in half lengthwise and scrape out and discard the seeds. Place the squash halves, cut sides down, on the prepared baking sheet. Bake until tender throughout, about 40 minutes. Test for doneness with a sharp knife or thin skewer; it should meet no resistance. Remove the squash from the oven and let cool. Using a spoon, scoop the flesh from the peel into a bowl. If any of the flesh sticks to the peel, just pull away the peel. You should have about 4 cups squash.

Reduce the oven temperature to 350 degrees F. Purée the squash in a food processor until smooth, or mash by hand using a fork. There should be no lumps. Leaving the squash in the food processor or bowl, add the ½ cup sugar, flour, milk, egg yolks, and ginger. Strain the sultanas, reserving them, and add the liquor to the squash mixture, then process or beat by hand until well mixed. Add the sultanas, pine nuts, and candied orange peel and mix until the ingredients are evenly distributed.

In a separate bowl, using an electric mixer, beat the egg whites with the salt until they begin to get foamy. Add the cream of tartar and continue to beat until the whites begin to form soft peaks, gradually adding the remaining 2 tablespoons sugar. Beat until the egg whites form peaks easily, but are not so stiff that they begin to separate into liquid and solid parts. Using a large rubber or plastic spatula, gently fold the egg whites into the squash mixture just until no white streaks remain. Pour the batter into the prepared baking pan.

Bake the cake until a knife inserted into the center comes out pretty clean and the top looks a little crusty, about 1 hour and 10 minutes. The cake should rise about 4 inches during baking. Remove from the oven and let cool on a rack for about 30 minutes. Run a knife around the inside edge of the pan to loosen the cake, then carefully invert onto a serving plate.

Let the cake cool completely before serving. It may be eaten the same day it is cooked or, better, the following day. The *budino* keeps well, refrigerated, for up to a week and freezes for up to 3 months.

Bread Pudding

pinza di pane

FOR 6 TO 8 PEOPLE

$1/4$ cup fine, fresh white bread crumbs

1 pound crust-free stale coarse country bread (about $1 1/4$ pounds with crust)

scant 4 cups milk

$1/3$ cup almonds, ground

$1/2$ cup walnuts, ground

$2/3$ cup sultanas

4 ounces very thinly sliced candied orange or other citrus peel or candied fruit

grated zest of 1 or 2 small navel oranges

2-inch piece fresh ginger or baby ginger, peeled and grated

7 tablespoons sugar, preferably superfine

2 tablespoons honey

$1/2$ teaspoon ground mace

tiny pinch of sea salt

5 extra-large eggs, separated

➤ *Pinza is an ancient Venetian dessert, made in endless permutations but always containing candied peel of orange or lemon. I like to keep the combination of flavors simple by leaving out the cinnamon, cloves, and rum that are often included. Instead, I fold in freshly grated ginger and a generous amount of fresh orange zest along with its candied counterpart. Use coarse country white bread that is a few days old, and is quite dry but not actually hard. Keep in mind that the better the bread, the better the pudding.*

Preheat the oven to 375 degrees F. Select a wide, shallow baking pan about 9 by 12 inches and 2 inches deep. If it is too deep, the pudding will be too moist in the center. If the pan is one that can double as the serving vessel, all the better. Grease the pan generously with butter. Sprinkle the bread crumbs into the pan evenly, then tilt the pan to coat the entire surface with a uniform layer. Tap out any excess and set aside.

Shred the coarse country bread finely. This can be done carefully in a food processor—the goal is fine shreds, not crumbs. In a large bowl, combine the shredded bread and the milk and let soak for 10 to 15 minutes. Use a wooden spoon to stir the mixture occasionally. Add the nuts, sultanas, candied peel, orange zest, ginger, sugar, honey, mace, and salt and mix well. In a separate bowl, beat the egg yolks lightly until blended, then mix them into the bread mixture. In another large bowl, using an electric mixer, beat the egg whites until they begin to form peaks easily, but are not so stiff that they begin to separate into liquid and solid parts. Using a large rubber or plastic spatula, gently fold the whites into the bread mixture just until no white streaks remain.

Using the spatula, carefully transfer the batter to the prepared baking pan, taking care not to disturb the coating on the pan and smoothing the surface to ensure that the batter is poured at an equal depth throughout.

Bake until golden brown, about 40 minutes. Turn off the oven and leave the pudding inside for 10 to 15 minutes. Remove from the oven, let the pudding cool completely on a rack, and serve.

Sand Cake

torta sabbiosa

FOR 6 PEOPLE

$^3/_4$ cup fine polenta

$1^1/_2$ teaspoons baking powder

1 cup potato starch (see recipe introduction)

1 cup (2 sticks) unsalted butter, at room temperature

$1^3/_4$ cups granulated sugar

3 extra-large eggs at room temperature, separated

$^1/_3$ cup milk, warmed

2 teaspoons pure vanilla extract

$^1/_4$ teaspoon sea salt

confectioners' sugar for dusting

Torta sabbiosa *has a history of at least three hundred years. It is based on potato starch* (fecola di patate), *which is a staple in the Italian kitchen but not always easy to find in America. If necessary, substitute an equal amount of cake flour. This is a classic Italian cake, a culinary genre recognizable by its ease of making and a certain moist, dense, buttery character that calls for a strong, dark espresso or an effervescent dessert wine alongside.*

Preheat the oven to 350 degrees F. Select a shallow cake pan about 10 inches in diameter. Grease the pan generously with butter and dust completely with flour, tapping out any excess.

In a bowl, stir together the polenta and baking powder. Sift the potato starch into a separate bowl.

In a large bowl, using an electric mixer, cream the butter and sugar until they are quite light, almost frothy. Once the mixture reaches this point, beat in the egg yolks one at a time, then the milk and vanilla; continue to beat until the mixture is light and airy. Now beat in the polenta mixture thoroughly. Re-sift the potato starch into the batter and continue to beat until a smooth, consistent batter results, another 3 minutes or so.

In a separate bowl using clean beaters, beat together the egg whites and salt until they form peaks easily, but are not so stiff that they begin to separate. Using a large rubber or plastic spatula, gently fold the whites into the batter just until no white streaks remain. Pour the batter into the prepared pan.

Bake the cake until a skewer inserted into the center comes out clean, about 40 minutes. Turn off the oven and leave the cake inside for 10 minutes. This will allow additional evaporation of moisture. Remove the cake from the oven and let cool completely on a rack. Run a knife around the inside edge of the pan to loosen the cake. Remove the cake from the pan and place it on a serving plate. When the cake has cooled completely, dust the surface with confectioners' sugar, then serve.

Josie Fido's Chestnut Cake

torta di castagne

FOR 6 PEOPLE

50 plump fresh Italian chestnuts,
or canned or frozen and thawed peeled
imported Italian or French chestnuts

1 teaspoon kosher salt (if using fresh
chestnuts)

$^3/_4$ cup (1$^1/_2$ sticks) unsalted butter
at room temperature

1 cup sugar

5 eggs, separated

1 teaspoon pure vanilla extract

The first time I ate this cake was in Josie Fido's kitchen. Her husband, Franco, a Venice native and the world's expert on famed Italian dramatist Carlo Goldoni, heads Harvard's Italian Studies department. Their house on the Rhode Island coast reminds you that Venetians are happiest when breathing salt air. Josie's chestnut cake is similar to several very old Venetian recipes that I discovered in my research. In Venice, confectioners' sugar is usually sprinkled on the cake, and some old recipes call for rum to be drizzled over it after it cools. While peeling the chestnuts is a tedious task, the results are well worth the effort. Avoid dried-out chestnuts that show some mold. Canned French chestnuts, stocked in specialty-food stores or available by mail order (page 158), can be substituted, although their flavor won't match that of good fresh ones.

Preheat the oven to 375 degrees F. Generously butter a round 10-inch cake pan.

If using fresh chestnuts, rinse well. Place the nuts in a large saucepan and add cold water to cover and the salt. Bring to a boil over high heat and cook until they are tender, about 30 minutes; a knife should easily insert into the center of a chestnut. Remove from the heat and, while still warm, use a small paring knife to peel off the shell and any traces of the bitter shell membrane. Keep the chestnuts immersed in the hot water until you are ready to peel each one. If they cool, peeling will be impossible. When all the chestnuts are peeled, grind them in a food processor or food mill.

In a large bowl, using an electric mixer, cream the butter and sugar until light. Add the ground chestnuts and beat until well mixed. Beat the egg yolks and vanilla into the chestnut mixture.

In another large bowl, beat the egg whites until they form peaks easily, but are not so stiff that they begin to separate into liquid and solid parts. Using a large rubber or plastic spatula, gently fold the whites into the chestnut mixture just until no white streaks remain. Pour the batter into the prepared pan.

Bake until a knife inserted into the center comes out clean, 25 to 30 minutes. Remove the cake from the oven and let cool completely on a rack. Run a knife around the inside edge of the pan to loosen the cake. Remove the cake from the pan and place it on a serving plate.

Crumb Cookies

sbrisolone

MAKES ABOUT 36 COOKIES

1 $^1/_8$ cups blanched almonds

2 $^1/_2$ cups cake flour

$^3/_4$ cup sugar

$^1/_8$ teaspoon sea salt

$^2/_3$ cup unsalted butter, melted

2 extra-large eggs, lightly beaten

1 teaspoon pure vanilla extract

$^1/_2$ teaspoon pure almond extract

Antiche Carampane restaurant in Venice is well known not only for its fish, but also for its sweets. Peter Wexler, a colorful New York stage set designer who lives in Venice half the year, has adopted the famous trattoria—or they have adopted him—and he has sent me Piera Agopyan's dessert recipes from time to time. These cookies are very simple; not even a mixer is required. They are plain in appearance but are very good, especially for breakfast.

Preheat the oven to 375 degrees F. Spread the almonds on a baking sheet. Slide the sheet into the oven and bake the almonds until they are a light tan, about 5 minutes. Remove the almonds from the oven and transfer them to a cutting board to cool. Chop the almonds roughly and set them aside.

In a large bowl, stir together the flour, sugar, and salt with a wooden spoon. Mix in the butter, nuts, eggs, and vanilla and almond extracts. The texture of the dough will be crumbly. With your hands, form the dough into a ball. Cover it with plastic wrap and chill for at least 2 hours or up to overnight.

Preheat the oven to 350 degrees F. Butter a large baking sheet or 2 smaller ones. Form the dough into balls, each about the size of an apricot, and place them on the prepared baking sheet(s), spacing them about 1½ inches apart. With your fingers, press down on each ball to flatten it into a disk. The size of the dough balls can be smaller if you want thinner cookies. If making smaller cookies, they can be spaced closer together on the baking sheet.

Bake the cookies until lightly golden on top and slightly browned on the bottom, 25 to 30 minutes, depending on how thick you formed them. Transfer the cookies to racks to cool. Once cooled, *sbrisolone* can be stored in airtight containers at room temperature for up to 2 weeks.

Cornmeal Cookies from the *Eolo*

*zaletti al'*Eolo

MAKES 40 COOKIES

1 cup dried currants

1 3/4 cups fine polenta (see recipe introduction)

1/2 cup (1 stick) plus 1 tablespoon unsalted butter at room temperature

2 extra-large eggs

1 cup sugar

1/2 teaspoon sea salt

2 tablespoons rum or cognac

finely grated zest of 1 large lemon

2 1/2 cups unbleached flour

1/2 cup pine nuts, lightly toasted

milk, if necessary

Here is a traditional Venetian cookie, the name of which derives from giallo, *"yellow," the color imparted to the dough by the polenta. A glass of sparkling Prosecco and a basketful of* zaletti (zaéti *in Venetian dialect) and other traditional Venetian cookies greeted me when I first boarded Mauro Stoppa's historical sailboat, the Eolo, in the port of Chioggia. Mauro kindly gave me this recipe. For the best results, use only finely ground polenta. To duplicate the type used in Venice for these cookies, pulverize the polenta in a coffee grinder to achieve a very fine flour.*

143

Place the currants in a small bowl and cover with cold water. Soak until plump and soft, about 1 hour. Drain before adding to the dough.

In a bowl, using an electric mixer, beat together the polenta and butter until creamy. Cover the bowl and let the mixture rest for 15 minutes. Meanwhile, in a large bowl, beat the eggs with the sugar until they are pale. Add the salt, rum, and lemon zest and beat until well combined. Add the flour, a little at a time, until it is fully incorporated, then mix in the pine nuts and the currants. Finally blend in the butter-cornmeal mixture to form a unified dough. It should be firm, but soft enough to work easily. If it is too soft, add a little more flour. If it is too stiff, add a little milk. Form the dough into a ball, cover in plastic wrap, and chill for about 2 hours.

Preheat the oven to 350 degrees F. Lightly grease 1 or 2 baking sheets with butter, depending on how many racks you have in the oven.

Sprinkle a work surface with flour. Roll the dough into long ropes about 3/4 inch in diameter and cut them into logs about 2 inches long. Work each log a bit in the palm of your hand to shape into small oval loaves. As each cookie is formed, place it on the prepared baking sheet(s). Space the cookies about 1 inch apart.

Bake the cookies until they are lightly golden on top and slightly browned on the bottom, about 20 minutes, depending on how thick you formed them. Transfer the cookies to racks to cool. Repeat to make the remaining cookies. Once cooled, *zaletti* can be stored in airtight containers at room temperature for up to 4 weeks.

Fried Carnival Pastries

galàni

FOR 6 PEOPLE

generous 2 cups unbleached flour

2 tablespoons cold unsalted butter, cut into small pieces

3 extra-large eggs

3 tablespoons granulated sugar

$1/4$ teaspoon sea salt

$1/4$ cup dry white wine, such as Soave, or grappa

corn oil for deep-frying

confectioners' sugar for dusting

 These thin pasta fritters are inescapable in the repertoire of Italian sweets, particularly at carnival time. The best pastries of the genre are very crisp and so delicately thin that they are in essence vaporoso, "like vapor," as Ranieri Da Mosto describes them in Il Veneto in cucina. *The dough should always incorporate wine or some kind of liquor, as it causes the pastries to fry up crisply and makes them light. Another rule is to roll out the dough as thin as possible. It takes great practice, strength, and skill to do this. I always use a hand-cranked pasta machine, passing the dough through the rollers set on the last notch to make it as thin and delicate as possible.*

To make by hand, sift the generous 2 cups flour into a bowl. Using your fingers or a pastry blender, work in the butter pieces until the mixture is the consistency of coarse meal. Turn the mixture out onto a large, floured pastry board or similar work surface. Using your fingers, make a well in the center of the mound. In a bowl, stir together the eggs, granulated sugar, salt, and wine with a fork until blended. Pour the mixture into the well and, using the fork and always stirring in the same direction, draw the dry ingredients into the wet ingredients. When a pliable dough begins to form, set the fork aside and work the dough with your hands. If it is too soft, sprinkle in more flour a little at a time. The dough should be workable, but not too stiff.

To make in a food processor, put the flour and butter into the processor and pulse until the butter has been transformed into crumblike pieces. Add the eggs, granulated sugar, salt, and wine and process until a smooth, uniform dough forms.

Divide the dough into 4 equal portions. Work with 1 portion at a time, keeping the other portions covered with a clean, slightly damp kitchen towel. On the floured pastry board, roll out the dough paper-thin—the thinner, the better. Alternatively, divide the dough into 8 equal portions and roll out each portion into the thinnest strip possible on a hand-cranked pasta machine: Start out at the widest setting and pass the dough through each consecutive setting once, ending with the thinnest setting. If the dough sticks, dust it lightly with flour before passing it through the rollers.

Using a fluted pastry wheel or a knife, cut the dough strip into rectangles about 2 by 3 inches. Make a horizontal cut in the center of each rectangle; this helps them fry evenly. Spread the rectangles out on clean, dry kitchen towels. Cover them with more clean, dry kitchen towels. Roll out and cut the remaining dough portions.

Into a deep skillet, pour corn oil to a depth of about 2 inches and heat over high heat until a scrap of dough dropped into the hot oil sizzles upon contact. Add the dough rectangles, a few at a time, to the hot oil. Do not crowd the pan. There should be enough oil around each rectangle to allow quick and even cooking. Fry, turning once, until evenly golden on both sides, about 2 minutes. Adjust the heat if the pastries are browning too quickly. Using a wire skimmer, transfer the pastries to paper towels to drain. You can stack them, but put paper towels between the layers to absorb the excess oil.

When all of the pastries are fried, let them cool completely, then dust generously with confectioners' sugar before serving.

Store the galàni in tightly sealed tins at room temperature for up to 3 weeks.

Every region and locality have their ways of making these sweet fried pastries. Even neighboring countries—Greece, Hungary, the Slavic countries, and others—make similar sweets. The galàni of Verona and Venice are particularly evocative because they are connected with carnival time, when they are stacked up in the windows of all the pastry shops in beautiful displays. What distinguishes the Veneto's galàni from those of other regions is their shape: large rectangles with a slash in the middle. Soave, one of the area's wines, is used in the many versions made in Verona and Venice, while in areas such as Bassano del Grappa and Conegliano, locally produced grappa goes into the dough.

POETIC PLACES
FOR SLEEPING AND EATING

soste degna de menzione

Venice has many famous and elegant hotels that well deserve their reputations. They are listed in travel guides and head the rosters of every travel agent. Many of them have fascinating histories or were once the residences of renowned literati, artists, and other famous personages. The great hotels have heady views of the city's distinctive facades, its monuments, and its canals. Web sites now enable you to know and see something of these landmark hotels in an instant. Simply put, a selective directory of hotels in Venice and the Veneto is not necessary. Nonetheless, I have assembled this one of some of the places I've been that are particularly notable for their celebrity, charm, or uniqueness, across the spectrum of price categories.

Giorgione, Cannaregio S.S. Apostoli, 4587, Venice. Tel: 041.52.25.810. Fax: 041.52.39.092. E-mail: giorg@doge.it. This elegant sixty-eight-room hotel (three stars) is one of my favorites in Venice for its location in a more intimate, if bustling, part of the city amid beautiful shops and even a grocery.

Gritti Palace Hotel, Campo Santa Maria del Giglio, San Marco, 2467, Venice. Tel: 041.79.46.11. Fax: 041.52.00.942. U.S. tel: 212.935.9540 or 800.221.2340. The Gritti Palace is one of the few hotels with the exclusive five-star rating. It is housed in a fifteenth-century palace over-looking one of the most picturesque stretches of the Grand Canal. The Gritti is particular about who its guests are—no organized groups are accepted—and it has always catered to famous literati and still does. You can have breakfast, lunch, dinner, or cocktails on the terrace overlooking the water, take shuttles to its sister hotel on the Lido, the Excelsior, which has a beach and a swimming pool, and be assured every comfort and consideration shown to the more celebrated guests who stay there.

Le Garzette Azienda Agrituristica, Lungomare Alberoni, 32, Mallamocco-Venice (on the Lido). Tel/fax: 041.73.10.78. Unique in Venice, this is a charming site of rustic agricultural tourism with an excellent trattoria. The two-bedroom suite on the top floor has a 360-degree view, which takes in both the lagoon and the Adriatic. This special little place fills up many months in advance, so call (if you speak Italian) or fax (if you don't) to reserve. You will be asked to wire a 50-percent deposit.

Locanda Cipriani, Torcello-Venice. Tel: 041.73.01.50. Fax: 041.73.54.33. E-mail: locandacipriani@italy.net. This famous inn on Torcello has four rooms for overnight guests. Reservations must be made well in advance. See restaurant section for dining information.

THE VENETO

Due Torri Baglioni, Piazza Sant'Anastasia, 4, Verona. Tel: 045.59.50.44. Fax: 045.80.04.130. A splendid ninety-one-room hotel in the rare five-star category, this was once the guest palace of the ruling family of Verona, the Scaligeri. The rooms are furnished in the period style of the hotel and have every convenience. In central Verona near the Adige River, within a five-minute walk of the bustling Piazza delle Erbe.

Hotel Grande Italia, Rione S. Andrea, 597 (Piazzetta Vigo), Chioggia (Venezia). Tel: 041.40.05.15. Fax: 041.40.01.85. A stately four-star hotel built in 1914 and newly restored. If you can get a room on the lagoon side, you will see the bustling port city, the actual fishing center for Venice, from your window. If lacking some charm, the rooms are pleasant and spacious, with all comforts. The city's open air market is set up right outside the front door.

AGRITURISMO IN THE VENETO

Farm vacations are a fast-growing cottage industry in Italy. A good source for locating *agriturismo* accommodations in the Veneto is *Veneto* (English edition), a guidebook published by the Touring Club of Italy. Touring Club Italiano, Corso Italia 10, 20122 Milan. Web site: www.touring club.it.

EATING OUT IN VENICE
AND THE VENETO

Venetians are prone to eating out rather than cooking. Venetian writer Paolo Lanapoppi, a keen observer of his native city, categorizes the city's popular fish trattorias that are by and large unknown to tourists as "false poor." They are typically busy, noisy, and informal, but the fare offered is cooked with great skill and pride. The good establishments are so popular among locals that it can be a challenge to be seated without reservations.

The following is a personal list of good places for authentic regional cooking in Venice and the Veneto. Most restaurants close one day every week, and reservations are advisable. If you are dining out in Venice, ask for directions when you call, as many addresses can be difficult to find. Many restaurants in Venice are open all year, but some close during winter. Restaurants near the ski resorts of Belluno close in spring and early summer.

These directories are by no means representative of the region's finest restaurants. Rather, they are lists of some of the places where I have enjoyed eating, that serve typical local cooking, or, in the case of a few establishments, deserve a visit because of a well-earned legendary status. Also listed are a few *osterie*, wine bars, where travelers particularly interested in wine will find an extraordinary selection from the region. Most *osterie* offer food as well; those listed serve good traditional fare.

RESTAURANTS IN VENICE   **Alla Maddalena,** on the garden island of Mazzorbo-Venice. Tel: 041.73.01.51. It is good to know that there is a trattoria on this bucolic island, which is otherwise used for growing artichokes.

Antiche Carampane, San Paolo, 1911, Rio Teradelle Carampane, Venice. Tel: 041.52.40.165. In 1358, the noble Rampani family donated some of their holdings to the Republic of Venice in order to establish a district in the city for women who made their living on the streets. One of the buildings donated is now home to this charming trattoria. The friendly Bortoluzzi family, who run it with love and pride, serve authentic Venetian cooking. The restaurant has an enchanting location right at the foot of the Ponte delle Tette (Bridge of the Breasts).

Busa alla Torre, Campo Santo Stefano, 3, Murano-Venice. Tel: 041.73.96.62. It is not easy to find a place that offers authentic cooking on Murano, where tourists typically flock to buy the decorative glass objects for which the island is famous. This informal restaurant, open only for lunch, serves typical local dishes.

Caffè Floridian, Procuratie Nuove, Venice. This is the oldest café in Venice, virtually intact since the eighteenth century with few compromises to the original style of decor. Tables are set in front of the café, which faces Piazza San Marco. If you sit there, eating alfresco, you'll no doubt understand why the Venetians call the piazza "the most elegant living room in Europe." A counter inside the café offers bar food at a reasonable cost. The prices rise meteorically in the lacquered rooms behind the windows. No reservations are necessary for the bar seats.

Da Romano, Burano-Venice, on the main and only thoroughfare. Tel: 041.73.00.30. Da Romano is the best-known restaurant on this enchanting island and one of Venice's best restaurants for fish. Romano Barbero founded it many years ago, and his family still manages the splendid "white glove" establishment that has served everyone from Stravinsky and Queen Elizabeth to Einstein, Gide, Hemingway, and Elizabeth David. Famous guests are asked to sign a guest book and include their comments. It is an interesting read. Professor Franco Fido, chairman of the Italian Studies department at Harvard and a native Venetian, sent me to Da Romano for the first time. The best idea, he said, is to go to the island early and plan to spend the whole day. Have lunch at one o'clock, then, in the late afternoon, hop on the ferry for nearby Torcello to have a late dinner at Locanda Cipriani.

Harry's Bar, Calle Vallaresso, 1323, Venice. Tel: 041.52.85.777. Fax: 041.52.08.822. Much has been written about Harry's Bar, once the salon of European and American writers and artists and the calling place of celebrities. That it is a "must" on the tourist route doesn't take away from its aura or the excellence of its food. Harry's Bar serves everything from Italian sandwiches and snacks to full-scale Italian and Venetian dinners.

Locanda Cipriani, 30012 Torcello-Venice. Tel: 041.73.01.50. Fax: 041.73.54.33. E-mail: locandacipriani@italy.net. Once an *osteria* that stocked wine, olive oil, and grappa, the *locanda* was transformed by Giuseppe Cipriani into an exclusive restaurant. It has passed down to Cipriani's nephew Bonifacio Brass and his mother, Carla Cipriani. Hemingway came here to eat *sole à la meunière* with curried rice and

Men are spending too much time eating and drinking and gambling in wine bars, leaving wives and children to starve at home. . . .

—Venice's Council of Ten, 1571, via Carole Rifkind

French wines. The food is refined and the setting enchanting, especially in the evening when the fog rolls in off the lagoon. It still serves sole. One memorable version was topped with sautéed *castraure*, the local baby artichokes.

Osteria Penzo, Calle Larga Bersaglio, 30015 Chioggia (Venice). Tel: 041.40.09.92. The restaurant is a few steps away from the Hotel Grande Italia (see page 147). Come here for genuine local cooking. Everything is freshly made, from the tagliatelle to the delicious biscotti.

Trattoria alle Garzette, Lungomare Alberoni, 32, Mallamocco-Venice. Tel/fax: 041.73.10.78. The owners serve organic vegetables and farm products from their garden and of their own production. This charming site of agricultural tourism (see page 147) will also serve the general public at its tables, by reservation.

Trattoria Corte Sconta, Castello 3886, Calle del Pestrin, Venice. Tel: 041.52.27.024. Fax: 041.52.27.513. Considered one of the best fish trattorias in Venice, the cooking at Corte Sconta is excellent. The place is always busy, so reservations must be made in advance.

CICHETI BARS IN VENICE

Many *cicheti* bars are informal and inexpensive wine bars *(bacari)* that offer a large variety of different labels by the glass. There are no reservations needed, hence no telephone numbers are listed. Hours of operation vary, but *cicheti* bars are typically open from 11:00 A.M. to 2:00 P.M., and from 5:00 P.M. to 8:00 P.M.

Enoteca al Volto, near the Goldoni Theater. As well as serving good *cicheti*, there is a wine cellar of far more than one thousand labels.

Cantina Do Mori, on Calle do Mori, past the archway off the main street to the Rialto. Terrific selection of *cicheti* and wines.

Mascarón, in the Campo Santa Maria Formosa. Recommended as the best place for *cicheti* by knowledgeable locals.

Osteria Antico Dolo, on Ruga Vecchia San Giovanni near the Rialto. Terrific variety of both *cicheti* and wines.

Antico Brolo, Corso Milano, 22, Padua. Tel: 049.66.45.55. Fax: 049.65.64.88. Excellent traditional provincial dishes offered in an elegant fifteenth-century building.

Baita Fraina, Via Fraina 1, Cortina D'Ampezzo (Belluno). Tel: 043.63.634. This is a chic ski resort town that comes alive in winter. The restaurant, elegant and lovely, serves both traditional and creative dishes.

Beccherie, Piazza Ancillotto, 11, in the historic center, Treviso. Tel: 042.25.40.871. This is where all the natives of Treviso tell you to go for the city's authentic cuisine. One can rely on finding genuine dishes of old Treviso here, including risottos of the season (not to be missed during the radicchio festival) and *stinco di maiale* (braised pork shins). The sweets are particularly beguiling. The place is always full of lively locals.

Biri, Piazza Statuto, 4, in the historic center, Bardolino. Tel: 045.72.10.873. This is where the town's shopkeepers, businesspeople, and the staff of the Istituto Alberghiero (the highly respected cooking and hotel school in town) can be found at lunchtime. The menu always has dishes of the season made in interesting but homespun ways, such as ravioli stuffed with arugula.

Calmiere, Ponte San Zeno, 10, in the historic center, Verona. Tel: 045.80.30.756. Fax: 045.80.31.900. Both the food and the setting here are traditional Veronese. On the menu are dishes that have even fallen out of favor in home kitchens. The restaurant is particularly pleasant during the harvest seasons, when Verona's fertile plains are bursting with beautiful vegetables and when, of course, the famous *vialone nano* rice of Isola della Scala is reaped. Here, the rice can be eaten at its prime, directly from the area's farms.

Cavallino Bianco, in the historic center, Treviso. Tel: 042.24.12.801.
Fernando Groppa, an ebullient and portly native with a handlebar mus-
tache, is a metaphor for his restaurant. It is timeless, buzzing with
activity, and full of atmosphere. Local dishes are served up with pride
and even a little fanfare, and there are also a few dishes of signor
Groppa's own *fantasia*. Groppa's wife, Caterina, runs the dining room
with cheer and charm. The restaurant makes traditional *soapa coada* of
squab, risottos of the season, *cinghiale in umido* (stewed boar), and
many other specialties. Some Venetian fish dishes are on the menu.
There is a veranda, marked at night by live torches all around, where one
can eat alfresco in warm weather.

Greppia, Vicolo Samaritana, 3, in the historic center, Verona.
Tel: 045.80.04.577. Fax: 045.59.50.90. Traditional Veronese dishes
served in an elegant setting not far from Piazza delle Erbe, Verona's
splendid main square. Go here for excellent *bollito misto* and the
Veronese sauces—*cren* and *pearà*—that go with it.

Il Capriolo, Via Nazionale, 108, Vodo di Cadore (Belluno).
Tel: 043.54.89.207. This fine restaurant offers extraordinary cooking
based on local traditions, but with refinements and a creative approach.
Owners Giacomo and Marina Gregorio have restored the building,
originally built by the Austrians for a post office, with attention to
historical detail.

La Loggia Rambaldi, Piazza Principe Amedeo, 7, Bardolino.
Tel: 045.62.10.091. This fashionable restaurant is housed in a sixteenth-
century building belonging to Contessa Guerrieri-Rizzardi, whose estate
is next door. Its location is virtually on Garda's lakefront. Use of local
ingredients, fish in particular, is a highlight of the cooking. During the
high tourist season, the chef indulges in some interesting creative
dishes along with traditional specialties.

Monaco Sport Hotel, Santo Stefano di Cadore (Belluno).
Tel: 043.54.20.440. Fax: 043.56.2218. Web site: www.monacosporthotel.com.
Named as such because it is surrounded by facilities for skiing, mountain

climbing, and other outdoor sports in a beautiful valley not far from the border of Friuli. Sergio de Candido runs the family-owned hotel-restaurant with an eye toward continuing a tradition of excellent local cooking. Interesting dishes include roasted *capriolo* (roe deer) with polenta, roasted pork fillet wrapped in *speck*, and venison stew served with a mountain of radicchio.

Osteria del Duca, Via Arche Scaligere, 2, in the historic center, Verona. Tel: 045.59.44.74. This rustic, boisterous, and casual *osteria*, located in the house where Romeo is said to have lived, serves terrific typical food, including donkey and horse meat, and is always mobbed at the lunch hour, so get there close to one o'clock.

Remo, Località Ca'Impenta, 14 (exit for Vicenza west), Vicenza. Tel: 044.49.11.007. The celebrated restaurant in a bucolic and rustic country setting serves traditional provincial cooking.

Le Zie Trattoria, 172 Seventh Avenue at 20th Street, New York, New York 10011. Tel: 212.206.8686. Fax: 212.924.9984. Located in the Manhattan neighborhood of Chelsea, this trattoria, owned by native Venetian Claudio Bonotto, offers excellent authentic Venetian food.

Remi, 145 West 53rd Street, New York, New York 10019. Tel: 212.581.4242. Fax: 212.581.8182. From Mestre (Venice), Francesco Antonucci is the master behind the impeccable cooking in this stunning restaurant designed by Adam Tihany. Here, Americans can eat the best Venetian dishes cooked in true Venetian style, such as *branzino* (sea bass) and *sardele in saor* (sweet-and-sour sardines). A preview of the menu can be found in Antonucci's fine cookbook, *Venetian Taste*, published by Abbeville Press. The restaurant is not far from Manhattan's theater district.

FESTIVALS

sagre

Perhaps the most dazzling festivals of all are those in Venice. The first *sagra* arose to celebrate the victory of Venice over Istrian pirates, who, for centuries, had raided the lagoon islands and kidnapped Venetian women. The historic event is still celebrated today. Unique to Venice are the regattas in which colorful local rivalries of gondoliers make a picturesque show. At other festivals, the Grand Canal is filled with restored historic gondolas and other boats and floats, all decorated lavishly with colors and lights.

The *Festa della Sensa* (Ascension), celebrated on the second Sunday in May, is perhaps the most famous and dramatic of all Venetian festivals. In another splendid Venetian festival, the *Festa della Rendentore*, boats of all kinds, festooned and lit up beautifully, fill the lagoon with music and song. During the celebrations, boaters throw picnics and lavish dinners on board.

FEBRUARY

Venice: While the origins of *Carnevale* date back to pagan rituals, the celebration was never the mass spectacle of today until the 1970s, when the city revived the tradition to promote off-season tourism. It has become a strange juxtaposition of ancient and modern, as costumed revelers wearing Renaissance costumes and wigs mingle with those wearing Disney masks. Pastry shop windows are stacked high with fascinating arrays of traditional sweets, many of which are reserved for carnival time.

Verona: *Venerdì Gnoccolare* (Gnocchi Friday) is a centuries-old celebration of potato gnocchi initiated by a procession in fourteenth-century costume that winds through the various quarters of the city. The colorful parade, which includes floats, bands, minstrels, costumed walkers on stilts and other performers, ends in Piazza San Xeno, where gnocchi are served to the crowds. The event takes place on the last Friday of Carnevale.

MARCH

Torri: Olive oil festivals begin in March and last until early spring.

APRIL

Teolo: An annual festival in celebration of potato gnocchi.

Venice: April 25, Feast of San Marco (Saint Mark), patron saint of Venice. During the times of La Serenessima, the doge initiated the saint's day with a course of *risi e bisi* (rice and peas), the most celebrated of all Venetian dishes.

MAY **Bassano del Grappa:** First Sunday, a *sagra* in celebration of the white asparagus of the region. Competitions are held for the best asparagus grown, and local restaurants serve it up.
Cavallino: On the first Sunday, a regatta is held during the day, and in the evening the local white asparagus is eaten to celebrate its season.
Venice: Second Sunday, the marriage ceremony of Venice with the sea (see facing page).

JUNE **Marostica:** First Sunday, *sagra* for the famous cherries of the region.

JULY **Garda:** Mid-July, festival of the *sardellate* fish of Lake Garda. Boats are festooned with lights and decorations. Sardines are fished, fried, and eaten.
Venice: Third week, *Festa del Redentore* celebrates the end of the plague in 1576. Floating feasts on boats and gondolas in the lagoon and a fireworks display are the festivities.
Verona: Opera and ballet festival.

AUGUST **Marniga:** In mid-August, the lovely feast of Saint Rocco. This festival was established in 1836, when the town named Saint Rocco the patron saint against cholera. All the streets are adorned with wreaths of bay leaves, and after the religious rituals and blessings, there is a festival at which local foods are sold in the central piazza.

SEPTEMBER **Bardolino:** End of September to the beginning of October, grape festival.
San Zeno: End of the month, livestock fair.
Soave: Second and third Sundays in September, a *sagra* celebrating the town's namesake wine.
Venice: First Sunday, *Regata Storica,* a historic regatta on the Grand Canal marking the end of the summer holiday. A show of restored antique gondolas carrying Venetians in historic costumes begins the event, and a race is held (see Festivals introduction).

OCTOBER

Bardolino: End of September to the beginning of October, grape festival.
Limone: Olive oil festival.
Santo Stino di Livenza (Venice): Third weekend, Feast of Autumn Flavors.
Teolo: Second Sunday, a chestnut *sagra* at which traditional local dishes are made.

NOVEMBER

Bardolino: Beginning of the month, a festival of the new wines.
Montagnana: November 25, Feast of Santa Caterina. Also the occasion of an annual market display of Montagnana's famous prosciutti.
San Giorgio Valpolicella: Third weekend, a festival based on ancient local tradition. Fava bean soup is made communally in the historic center and eaten with chestnuts of the season and the local red wine.
Sant'Ambrosio di Valpolicella: November 7, a festival celebrating fava beans, associated with immortality.
San Zeno: Chestnut festival.
Venice: On the last Sunday, the feast of the Madonna della Salute is initiated at the baroque church of Santa Maria della Salute, erected in honor of the Virgin Mary in recognition of her help in ending the plague in 1630. A dish of the time, *la castradina* (smoked salted mutton with cabbage), is served in trattorias throughout the city.

DECEMBER

Castelfranco Veneto: Radicchio Festival
Treviso: Restaurants throughout the city cook the radicchio in all kinds of dishes in a market under the arch of a Renaissance palazzo.

COOKING CLASSES
AND WINE COURSES

IN THE UNITED STATES

Anna Teresa Callen Italian Cooking School, 59 West 12th Street, New York, New York 10011. Tel: 212.929.5640. Anna Teresa Callen is a native Italian who lived for many years in Padua, in the Veneto. She is the author of numerous books about Italian cooking, an authority on regional Italian cooking, and a charismatic and engaging teacher.

La Vera Cucina, Julia della Croce's Italian Cooking School, Rockland County, New York. Tel: 845.634.3172. Web site: www.juliadellacroce.com. E-mail: julia@juliadellacroce.com. Specializing in regional Italian cooking. Instruction by award-winning cooking teacher Julia della Croce and celebrated guest cooking teachers. Classes in wine appreciation. Referral service for professional Italian chefs, Italian food consultants, Italian food and travel photographers, and Italian food, wine, and olive oil experts.

The Magazine of La Cucina Italiana Cooking School, 230 Fifth Avenue, New York, New York 10001. Tel: 212.725.8764, or 888.742.2373. E-mail: piacere@earthlink.net. Demonstration classes with well-known Italian chefs and cookbook authors. Classes in wine and olive oil appreciation.

IN ITALY

To Italy with Julia. Tel: 845.634.3172. Web site: www.juliadellacroce.com. E-mail: julia@juliadellacroce.com. Unique culinary and cultural tours of Italy with Julia della Croce, award-winning author and teacher.

MAIL-ORDER SOURCES
FOR VENETO PRODUCTS

Buon Italia
Chelsea Market
75 Ninth Avenue
New York, New York 10011
Tel: 212.633.9090
Fax: 212.633.9717
Web site: www.buonitalia.com
High-end regional Italian and Veneto food specialties and hard-to-find Italian food imports. Mail order, Internet, retail, and restaurant trade sales. Orders shipped.

Coluccio & Sons
1220 60th Street,
Brooklyn, New York 11219
Tel: 718.436.6700
Italian and Veneto food specialties. Product list available. Orders shipped.

D'Artagnan
280 Wilson Avenue
Newark, New Jersey 07105
Tel: 800.327.8246
Fax: 973.465.1870
E-mail: email@dartagnan.com
Meat specialty products. Organic meats, exotic meats, smoked and preserved meats, sausages. Phone, mail, or Internet order. Free catalog available.

Dean & DeLuca
Mail-Order Department
560 Broadway
New York, New York 10012
Tel: 212.431.1691 or 800.221.7714
Kitchen equipment; Italian specialty foods. Catalog available.

DiPalo's Italian Fine Foods
206 Grand Street
New York, New York 10013
Tel: 212.226.1033
Open since 1925, this old-world grocer in New York City's Little Italy (according to Louie DiPalo, the "twenty-first region of Italy") carries every Italian food specialty exported. Too many products to list, but they will ship anything ordered by phone.

Fante's
1006 South Ninth Street
Philadelphia, Pennsylvania 19147-4798
Tel: 215.922.5557 or 800.44FANTE
Web site: www.fantes.com
One of America's oldest and best-stocked kitchenware companies. Solid copper polenta pots and cornmeal for polenta are sold.

Gallo Brokerage
93 Willow Street
Wilkes-Barre, Pennsylvania 18702
Tel: 570.882.9743
Fax: 570.822.6622
Broker for Italian specialty foods supplying distributors and importers.

Sur la Table
Catalog Division
1765 Sixth Avenue South
Seattle, Washington 98134-1608
Tel: 800.243.0852
Web site: www.surlatable.com
Fine kitchen equipment, including copper paiolo pots for cooking polenta. Catalog available.

ACKNOWLEDGMENTS

Every cookbook has its page of perfunctory acknowledgments, usually saying something to the effect that the writer is grateful to someone for eating their experiments throughout the testing. I have even more for which to be thankful. Writing a cookbook like this, the very aim of which is to draw readers into other people's lives, means relying on people I've never known to take me into their homes or restaurant kitchens; to tell me, a perfect stranger, about themselves and their mothers (because they usually learn to cook from them); and what they eat and why. Many of the people I thank were more generous than I could have ever expected.

The Veneto is a vast region with much ground to cover, which made my task a challenging one. I am thankful indeed for the kindnesses of many people on both sides of the ocean: To Giovanni Nonne and his family for putting his hotel at my disposal in Borca di Cadore. To Paolo Destefanis for going beyond the photographer's assignment to make my job easier. To Ester Chines for traveling from Tuscany to Venice to help with photography. To Flavia Destefanis for her editorial work in Italian and for connecting me to the Veneto in so many ways. To Franco Fido and his wife, Josie, for the advice on travels to Venice and for the extraordinary cooking. To Bill Marsano for so many kindnesses besides advice on the wine chapter. To Paolo Lanapoppi for his invaluable advice in Venice. To Claudio Pro and his wife, Rita, for wonderful recipes and entertaining afternoons. To Salvatore and Renza for letting me in their busy kitchen and permitting our photography at Le Garzette. To Mauro Stoppa for extraordinary generosity with advice and hospitality on the *Eolo* and in Chioggia and to Antonio Mazzetti of the *Eolo* for his contributions. To Peter Wexler for the delightful stories and for transcribing and faxing recipes from Piera Agopyan in Venice, and to Piera and Antiche Carampane for those recipes. To Nicoletta Polo for her insights about Venice. To Giacomo Gregorio of Il Capriolo for the fascinating history lesson. To Dottor Giorgio Lulli, Augusto Marchini, Maria Woodley, and Jacqueline Greaves of ICE in New York and Verona for help with research. To Dr. Ernesto Ferran for many kindnesses and for introducing me to Francesco Antonucci. To Franceso Antonucci for the numerous delicious meals at Remi in New York and for his extraordinary generosity, including the ten pounds of *vialone nano* rice. To Claudio Bonotto of Le Zie for taking time to meet with me. To Gian Andrea Tinazzi of the Tinazzi Vineyards for generous help with research. To Contessa Guerrieri-Rizzardi for her hospitality in Bardolino. To Fabrizio DeVenosa and his wife, Elisabetta, of La Loggia Rambaldi in Bardolino for devoting an entire afternoon to preparing recipes for tasting and photography. To Luca Fasoli for sharing his final thesis on fish at the Instituto Alberghiero in Bardolino. To Anna Teresa Callen for translating the Venetian text. To Anna Amendolara Nurse for help with research. To Thomas Melilli of Hotel Boite for assistance with research. To Carlo Pomaré of Hotel Boite for the generous gifts of books and help with research. To Sergio de Candido of Monaco Sport Hotel for the lesson on the cooking of Comèlico. To Clarisse Schiller for leads in Treviso. To Thomas Briccetti (in memoriam), Mauro Stoppa, and Bill Marsano for their kindnesses on the wine trail and to Paolo DeBortoli for the helicopter ride invitation over his Prosecco vines in Valdobbiadine. Thanks to Bertolli Olive Oil and Le Molisana Pasta for supplies. For help with recipe testing, I thank my mother, Flavia Destefanis; Diane Messina; Tom McQuade; Mitch Weinstien; Lana Santavicca; Linda Fraser; Michael Heinrich; and Nancy Pigg. I have special thanks to Annette Messina and Ernest Symanski not only for their remarkable generosity in testing many recipes meticulously, but also for sending me the perfectly packed, fresh samples so that I could taste.

INDEX

TABLE OF EQUIVALENTS

The exact equivalents in the following tables have been rounded for convenience.

Liquid/Dry Measures

U.S.	METRIC
¼ teaspoon	1.25 milliliters
½ teaspoon	2.5 milliliters
1 teaspoon	5 milliliters
1 tablespoon (3 teaspoons)	15 milliliters
1 fluid ounce (2 tablespoons)	30 milliliters
¼ cup	60 milliliters
⅓ cup	80 milliliters
½ cup	120 milliliters
1 cup	240 milliliters
1 pint (2 cups)	480 milliliters
1 quart (4 cups, 32 ounces)	960 milliliters
1 gallon (4 quarts)	3.84 liters
1 ounce (by weight)	28 grams
1 pound	454 grams
2.2 pounds	1 kilogram

Length

U.S.	METRIC
⅛ inch	3 millimeters
¼ inch	6 millimeters
½ inch	12 millimeters
1 inch	2.5 centimeters

Oven Temperature

FAHRENHEIT	CELSIUS	GAS
250	120	½
275	140	1
300	150	2
325	160	3
350	180	4
375	190	5
400	200	6
425	220	7
450	230	8
475	240	9
500	260	10